Praise for EVERYTHING IS HERE TO HELP **YOU**

"*Everything Is Here to Help You* is a brilliant synthesis of insight, guidance, warmth, and wisdom that will open the heart and calm the mind. I loved every word, and will keep it close to my bedside as it has so much to offer I want to be able to sip its sweet wisdom often. It's a gift to yourself to read it."

— Sonia Choquette, *New York Times* best-selling author of
*Your 3 Best Super Power*s

"Matt Kahn brilliantly nails it with *Everything Is Here to Help You*. By guiding us to see life as it really is, from a soul level, he reveals the phenomenal order of the Universe, our lives, and those things that challenge us, so that we may gain an upper hand, choosing to live deliberately and on purpose, loved and in love."

— Mike Dooley, *New York Times* best-selling author of
Infinite Possibilities and *Playing the Matrix*

"Somewhere in the dance between the ego and the soul is the truth of our wild ride here on earth. We are most in alignment and co-creative brilliance when the soul is driving the bus, but most of us are unwitting hostages while the ego drives us around revisiting all kinds of spots we'd rather not. Matt's beautiful book teaches us how to reassign the ego and elevate the soul. That is when our destiny, our true potential awakens—not just for the individual, but in service to the whole world. Highly recommended."

— Colette Baron-Reid, best-selling author of *Uncharted*

"I love Matt and I'm thankful for his existence.
Grab this book and change your world."

— Kyle Cease, *New York Times* best-selling author of
I Hope I Screw This Up

EVERYTHING
IS HERE
TO HELP
YOU

ALSO BY **MATT KAHN**

Whatever Arises, Love That:
A Love Revolution That Begins with You

EVERYTHING
IS HERE
TO HELP
YOU

FINDING THE GIFT IN LIFE'S
Greatest Challenges

MATT KAHN

HAY HOUSE, INC.
Carlsbad, California • New York City
London • Sydney • New Delhi

Published in the United States by: Hay House, Inc.: www.hayhouse.com®
Published in Australia by: Hay House Australia Pty. Ltd.: www.hayhouse
.com.au • *Published in the United Kingdom by:* Hay House UK, Ltd.: www
.hayhouse.co.uk • *Published in India by:* Hay House Publishers India: www
.hayhouse.co.in

Cover design: Amy Grigoriou • *Interior design:* Bryn Starr Best

Library of Congress has cataloged the earlier edition as follows:

Names: Kahn, Matt, author.
Title: Everything is here to help you : a guide to your soul's evolution / Matt Kahn.
Description: 1st Edition. I Carlsbad : Hay House, Inc., 2018.
Identifiers: LCCN 2017060614 I ISBN 9781401954956 (hardcover : alk. paper)
Subjects: LCSH: Spiritual life. I Spiritual healing.
Classification: LCC BL624 .K27 2018 I DDC 204/.4--dc23 LC record available at https://lccn.loc.gov/2017060614

Tradepaper ISBN: 978-1-4019-5497-0
E-book ISBN: 978-1-4019-5496-3
Audiobook ISBN: 978-1-4019-5565-6

10 9 8 7 6 5 4 3 2

1st edition, June 2018
2nd edition, June 2019

Printed in the United States of America

To my beloved Alexandra, this book was written as a celebration of our love to heal all hearts through the ecstasy of our sacred union.

To all empaths, lightworkers, and energetically sensitive beings who have been overwhelmed by the energies of others and wish to find true relief as we usher in a new spiritual paradigm for humanity, this book is for you.

CONTENTS

INTRODUCTION

AS THE ANCIENT SCRIPTURES SAY, "In the beginning, there was the Word."

This is a perfect way to describe my journey as an intuitive. I would find myself mentally resting in an open, blank space with the excitement of a child ready to open presents on Christmas morning. When the time was right, out of nowhere, words spoke through me as spontaneous streams of inspired wisdom. No matter how flawlessly it always worked out, each and every time, it always felt like I was standing at the threshold of one of life's most suspenseful and exhilarating encounters, supplied only with the clear impulse of each instinct and an irrefutable will to serve the well-being of every heart—often with just one auspicious hour to radically transform the life of someone I'd never met.

This has been the vivid testimony of my daily experience that I have been so blessed to explore over the past 14 years. Since following an instinct to walk out of college one crisp November afternoon, when I boldly declared the *Universe* my university of higher learning, I have been guided by an irrefutable force of inner knowing. It's an immaculate flow of insight that has used each of my personal experiences to be the teacher, empath, and intuitive healer that I never knew I was destined to become.

It always felt ironic to be a spontaneous source of clarity for others and yet totally in the dark as to where my own life was headed. In a journey that often feels like it began just yesterday, more than 13,000 healing sessions later I have become keenly familiar with how the spiritual path ebbs and flows, from one level of expansion to the next. It has provided me with a lengthy examination to understand why people who often begin a spiritual journey fail to find the true relief, unwavering peace, existential joy, and profound clarity that is here to be uncovered.

Throughout each session, I would listen with captivated interest to the feedback each person offered about various paths, transformational processes, healing modalities, and mystical approaches. It was as if the Universe was teaching me the ins and outs of an old spiritual paradigm I was here to help transform.

I remember so often hearing people talk about specific stumbling blocks or moments of confusion from their initial spiritual paths, and on the inside, most of it didn't make any bit of sense. If it weren't for the cascading stream of clarity that ran through my mind in response to any question or concern, I'd probably just sit across from each person in complete awe and disbelief.

As their questions and my intuitive responses provided a necessary dialogue to bring me up to speed on how most people pursued the healing, awakening, and transformation of reality, I began noticing themes emerging that revealed cracks throughout a crumbling, outdated, spiritual paradigm. This inspired an insatiable desire to provide each human being with the profound spiritual experiences I had been encountering throughout my life.

While a spiritual journey has always been a fundamental transition from ego to soul, I began to see how those in search of truth weren't necessarily exploring it from the soul's perspective. Instead, many facets of inner growth were explored from the *ego's* point of view. In my first book, *Whatever Arises, Love That*, I explained the nature of ego as the imaginary identity of an overstimulated nervous system. Such patterns of overstimulation get created in our early years of development by subconsciously believing we will be more *liked* by others if we are more *like* others. This creates a psychological cocoon of human conditioning for the soul to inhabit until it is ready to awaken and expand into the light of its highest potential. Suffice it to say, the ego is the limiting beliefs, self-defeating choices, and narrow viewpoints of dormant consciousness. As consciousness begins waking up, limiting beliefs dissolve, self-defeating choices no longer resonate, and narrow viewpoints are exchanged for more expansive perspectives.

The purpose of our evolution is to shift out of ego and into the brightness of the soul, but it is often misconstrued when we are under the impression that ego and soul are *separate*. While the ego and soul can exist as two different experiences, they are both aspects of an omnipresent Source of Divine Intelligence.

Such a truth highlights the interconnectedness of the Universe that unites *all things as one*, no matter how separate they seem or how much distance exists between them. While the ego is the soul in its most dormant state of incubation, the soul is a fully embodied expression of Source energy. Between these two aspects, a spiritual journey unfolds.

In order for a spiritual journey to offer the most rewarding experiences, the question remains: Is it being explored from the ego or from the soul's perspective?

If one pursues spiritual growth from the standpoint of ego, they are bound to remain in ego, no matter how much inner work they complete. If one learns how to evolve from the soul's perspective, more vivid experiences of life can occur. Since the soul is a conscious expression of Source energy, it resonates with a depth of clarity that is as harmonious, inclusive, and kind as it is direct, effective, and potent.

In response to meeting so many energetically sensitive beings, whose paths only seem to make them more doubtful, ashamed, and critical of themselves, I realized the importance of a heart-centered path to liberate our true innocent natures from any degree of spiritual bondage.

OUT OF THE INNER WAR

Everything Is Here to Help You is an emotionally supportive way of shifting out of the inner war of ego and into the illuminated presence of soul. Since the ego is the unconscious behavior of limiting beliefs, self-defeating choices, and narrow points of view, the "inner war" being resolved is an evolutionary necessity of integrating the ego, which helps us purge the patterns of human conditioning that often make us feel like victims of our circumstances, instead of pioneers of an awakening humanity.

To assist in ending the inner war in the most nurturing way, this book has been created to explore the most crucial levels of the soul's expansion with clarity and ease. From cultivating our highest Divine attributes and balancing out inner masculine and feminine energies, to transforming our relationships through the gifts of spaciousness and self-love, our journey together guides us beyond each sticking point and into the joy of our deepest heartfelt surrender.

This book also includes engaging questions to contemplate throughout each chapter, as well as energetically encoded mantras and "repeat after me" statements to activate and awaken life's unlimited potential.

While many insights offered throughout this book may seem to click magically into place, others may challenge layers of ego or the density of inner stagnation that may not be ready to be unraveled. With love leading the way, the ecstasy of venturing beyond all boundaries and barriers becomes less overwhelming, less exhausting, and more exciting and instinctive.

One compassionate step at a time, the truth of our eternal nature can be revealed, without needing to be anything else but exactly as we were born to be.

MAKING
SENSE OF
YOUR SOUL'S
JOURNEY

CHAPTER 1

ENDING
THE INNER
WAR

IN THIS NEW PARADIGM, our spiritual journey requires us to evolve from the soul's point of view. This is important, so the ego doesn't get reinvented with a more spiritually themed persona. If this occurs, we maintain the density of human conditioning but with newly discovered spiritual reasons to justify staying aligned with limiting beliefs, self-defeating choices, and narrow viewpoints.

Such a timeless undertaking always begins with ending the inner war of ego. No matter where we are in our journey, it is important to embrace the soul's wisest and most loving way of approaching this process. Otherwise, we are attempting to end the inner war with aggression, only to make our ego into a spiritual mask to wear or an enemy to oppose. One cannot resolve an internal conflict by being at odds with the parts that seem so conflicted. Therefore, it is essential that each milestone of our journey, including the ending of the inner war, be pursued with compassion.

When exploring a spiritual journey from the ego's perspective, it is natural to be excited about a variety of mystical subject matters, while seemingly less interested in embodying the highest qualities and embracing the most courageous decisions of a fully realized soul. If we listen to our ego, we venture toward a more empowered reality, while often going about such a goal in a fear-based or superstitious manner.

When guided by the negative reinforcement of our ego, goals remain positive, while our focus tends to obsessively scan for any shred of inner discord. This is much like someone who tirelessly works on a classic car in their garage for many years. While attempting to rebuild the perfect vehicle, somehow they never get around to taking it for a ride. Similarly, when we are guided by ego, it is common to live in a state of guardedness where the hope is to avoid the despair of emotional reactions and resist the temptation of getting caught in the tailspin of negative thinking.

Of course, only the ego fights, avoids, overcomes, or denies, so it becomes easy to see when an authentic spiritual journey has shifted into an odyssey of opposition. Whether you are fighting with your own fears, avoiding the gravity of painful feelings, attempting to unhook from the conditioning of your family too quickly, or working desperately to overcome the intensity of your most limiting thoughts, it is easy to get lost in ego.

It is true that as the soul steps forward, we no longer fight against ourselves and others, or resist the choices that call us forward into the reclaiming of our true spiritual power. These are the gifts we are blessed to receive as our inner war is brought to an end. As this occurs, we no longer resist any particular feeling, have any ancestral conditioning to resolve, or have any thoughts to reject. And yet, such a wondrous and surreal reality cannot be cultivated when we're focused on trying to avoid or control anything at all. From the soul's perspective, there is a much more direct way to evolve.

THE BEGINNING OF THE END

Ending the inner war occurs by integrating the ego from the soul's perspective. This is because the soul has tremendous reverence for the ego and its destiny of unraveling. It views ego as a sacred womb, where the soul resides in its most dormant stages of infancy until it is time to awaken for the well-being of all. When children are birthed from wombs, doctors are not trying to harm the mother or destroy the womb in order to bring a baby into the world. Therefore, as metaphorical mothers and midwives who are escorting the light of our souls into humanity, only the most harmonious approach can provide the relief we seek.

In the new spiritual paradigm, we do not oppose ego.

Instead, we are heart-centered anchors of a new humanity who have come to liberate the ego from cycles of self-imposed pain by returning it to Source in the most loving way.

When the soul awakens, it initially assists in the integration of ego by becoming aware of it. As we learn to become familiar with recurring patterns of ego, without judging it or buying into its beliefs and demands, the grip of inner conflict begins to loosen.

The soul is like a unique ray of light expressed from the sun of our one eternal Source. Simply by viewing the ego with loving compassion, the light of the soul begins to soften each harsh and rigid edge until each layer melts away.

Whenever we bring a greater interest of gentle attention to how the ego tends to function, its operating system can be deconstructed with peaceful resolve.

THREE ACTIVITIES OF EGO: WAR

To become aware of how our soul operates in the ego's most stagnant phase of incubation, we begin by recognizing the three activities of ego. Much like the predictable and reoccurring seasons we observe in nature, these activities represent the patterning that perpetuates life's most self-defeating beliefs and least desirable qualities.

While the instincts of fight, flight, and freeze are ingrained in our survival mechanism, the three activities of ego reveal the inner motivation that fuels each of these reactions into motion. They are the patterns of worry, anticipation, and regret.

ONE. *The Ego Always Worries.* The ego cannot exist without a sense of worry. It is rooted in a primal tendency to distrust the perfection of Divine Order. The ego is incapable of accepting its true identity as a pure and untainted expression of Source. Worry extends from fear. This occurs when the soul is building up the energetic momentum to expand, while incubating in its most dormant and often disempowered states of being. A core belief in ego is imagining how less worrisome it would be if only the terms and conditions of reality could be constantly changed to satisfy its liking.

Beliefs such as these tend to mislead so many people who may assume they will feel differently once their external reality changes. This supports the ego's primary belief that outside circumstances must shift before a better experience can be felt. While there are certainly moments in time when external changes are a necessary means of evolution, the tendency to insist that resolve must occur from the "outside in" is a pattern known as attachment.

When attached to external outcomes, our energy fields halt their ever-expanding trajectory. From this space of shutting down, the soul's expansion pauses—though it certainly cannot stop evolution, since everything in existence only occurs for the benefit of our journey.

As we gather the necessary experiences in ego to see through such limiting viewpoints, our energy fields are able to open up with greater awareness and renewed perspective—and to continue expanding.

Even though a pattern such as worry can be deeply painful when experienced, it surely plays a key role in our evolution. Beyond the physical and mental discomfort, its purpose is to create an energetic momentum that inspires our consciousness to awaken. This buildup of energy occurs as we oscillate between each activity of conditioning, like someone who must toss and turn in bed in order to awaken from a vivid dream they may not have known they were having.

T W O. *The Ego Needs to Anticipate.* The second activity of ego is anticipation. As ego steeps in worry, there is often something painful it anticipates. When lost in anticipation, the ego hopes to see impending inconveniences coming from such a distance that it can swiftly avoid any degree of frustration, pain, or loss.

It is also important to see how ego maintains unconsciousness, whether anticipating pain or awaiting moments of pleasure. This doesn't mean that looking forward to future events means you're lost in ego. It's simply a matter of noticing how much of your time is occupied waiting for something else to occur.

The tendency to live more in anticipation than in each moment at hand maintains the ego's attachment to believing that outside circumstances must change before life can feel different. When lost in anticipation, we tend to believe that however we envision future moments to unfold is exactly how things are going to turn out. This means the ego either needs outcomes to be exactly how they have been envisioned in order to be happy, or the ego steeps in fear, assuming the way it sees things is the only way life is meant to be. In either case, an attachment to outcome keeps us needing to assert control over reality, which further slows down the expansion of the soul.

As the inner war of ego unravels, things may or may not go as planned, but life always unfolds in whatever way guides us into higher levels of expansion.

THREE. *The Ego Must Regret.* A refusal to embrace the evolutionary benefits of however life unfolds is a pattern known as regret. This is the third activity of ego.

Instead of anticipating potential adversities to come, the ego often maintains a state of unconsciousness by looking back and casting blame at the people, places, or things it believes are the cause of its pain. Since the ego is the soul in its most dormant phase of expansion, it inherently feels left out, alone, abandoned, and betrayed by a Universe that only creates moments in time for the benefit of our growth. If the ego were to feel more connected and supported by the Universe, there would be no ego to notice it. This is because only the soul aligns with Source. Therefore, painful feelings of regret and disconnection signify a soul in an existential state of incubation, preparing for the arrival of its awakening consciousness.

In some cases, our regret can inspire us to look back to acknowledge the lessons, wisdom, and choices that were previously overlooked. But when we are dominated by the ego, regret is used to unconsciously hide from the potential threats in our daily lives. As part of ego's vicious cycle, regret anticipates worst-case scenarios to inspire the activity of worry. Once worry is set into motion, it uses regrets from the past to turn away from whatever it worries about anticipating.

Equally so, the ego can often use past moments of regret to project negative outcomes onto anticipations of the future to further the activity of worry.

So you see, this becomes a vicious cycle of worry, anticipation, and regret.

FROM INCUBATION TO EXPANSION

In examining the three activities of ego, we notice that its habitual tendency to oscillate between worry, anticipation, and regret maintains an unconscious state of incubation. This occurs until the soul has reached a critical threshold, at which point it is ready for the transformational milestones of a spiritual journey.

Looking at the first letter of each ego activity, we notice worry, anticipation, and regret spell the word *WAR*. This suggests that any degree of inner war or personal conflict is created out of a foundation of dormant consciousness. As the soul begins its evolutionary journey of shifting out of incubation into expansion, it is our willingness to notice these activities of ego with greater awareness that assists in the process.

Ending the inner WAR is much like an equation. It is what I refer to as the equation of "ARE":

Awareness + Resolution = Expansion

Many yearn for resolution without first developing the awareness that is essential for their highest spiritual growth. Others have become keenly aware of how worry, anticipation, and regret often influence their lives but are left without a way of knowing what to do next.

This is why the equation of ARE becomes an essential formula in ending the inner WAR.

To support the equation of ARE as a road map of evolution, the acronym "WE" is useful: "Word Embodied." As I like to say, "In the beginning, there was the Word, and the Word of Truth brought everything into existence."

Since each of us is a living expression of Source energy, WE are the holy Word Embodied in human form. WE have incarnated on an ever-expansive journey where Awareness and Resolution inspire the Expansion of the soul to remember, realize, and return to the ONE.

Since our Divine Source is all-knowing and all-loving, its presence shines in all to remind us of ONE, or Openness Never Excludes.

Word Embodied (WE)

Awareness + Resolution = Expansion (ARE)

Openness Never Excludes (ONE)

In other words, WE ARE ONE.

To help embody the insight of WE ARE ONE, please consider the wisdom of or repeat aloud the following statement:

I accept that the ego is the soul in its most dormant stages of incubation. It is not to be opposed, rejected, or denied, no matter how painful it may be when oscillating between patterns of worry, anticipation, and regret. I accept that I do not worry, anticipate, or regret for any of the reasons I may believe or have imagined. I am simply playing out these patterns as a way of building up momentum to inspire an awakening of consciousness.

In knowing it is so, I allow all aspects of the inner WAR to be healed and resolved, as I create more space for my soul to expand. I embrace my most profound healing in the name of love, knowing all that I resolve within assists in transforming each heart throughout, since WE ARE ONE. And so it is.

As we allow lifelong attachments to inner stagnation to melt away by repeating such a powerful statement, we may discover renewed levels of inner spaciousness and greater perspectives of clarity to assist in ending the inner war. In doing so, we are not condemning, judging, or denying ego, but freeing it from the incubation of inner stagnation by returning it to Source in the most heart-centered way.

CHAPTER 2

FREEDOM
FROM THE
SPIRITUAL
MICROSCOPE

WHILE 10 YEARS HAVE PASSED since an auspicious moment in time altered the course of my reality, I remember it as if it just occurred. There I was, standing in front of a full-length mirror in my bedroom, overcome by an impulse to look directly into my own reflection without turning away. It seemed like an existential standoff between everything I was taught about myself by the outside world and an inner knowing that refused to stay in the background any longer. As I looked into the depth of my own eyes, I could feel an intensity of impending revelation shaking within me. It was as if tiny hurricanes of energy were opening up within the cells of my body.

As this happened, the form I saw reflected in the mirror became less dense and began vibrating as a manifestation of pure light. I immediately saw very directly how the person I had taken myself to be was actually an expression of eternal radiance. Nothing about the person was wrong, insignificant, or even capable of blocking the light that I saw pulsating throughout me. In fact, it was at that moment that everything about my body, mind, and personality somehow felt whole, complete, and perfect. In what seemed like an instantaneous shift, I was experiencing the reality within the form. It unleashed a wellspring of harmony, respect, and reverence for all living creatures and sentient beings.

The light pulsating within me continued to expand outside of my body until everything in view and around me vibrated as one undivided reality. The peace was immense. The relief felt so natural and unwavering. I finally felt welcomed and at home with a profound truth that refused to go overlooked for even one moment longer. As I stared at the energy within the perceived boundaries of my body, I instinctively knew it to be the light of my soul.

While everything vibrated as one all-knowing and all-loving omnipresent field of light, the energy encompassing my body was seen as a unique way this spacious infinite field was expressing and exploring itself as a person named Matt.

It was at that moment I heard the following words flow through me: *I once was a person standing in a space and now I'm the space where a person stands.*

Instead of being a person considering the nature of the soul, I was the soul experiencing its own Divine nature while taking shape and form in a play of space and time. It wasn't as if this revelation made people, places, and things less relevant. In such a direct, irrefutable, and obvious way, I instinctively felt the aliveness of divinity in every form, as if I were dwelling in everything *all at once*. And yet, this "personal self" felt like it was equally created to offer the soul a unique vehicle for its ongoing cosmic adventures.

On that fateful Sunday afternoon, while standing in front of a mirrored closet in my bedroom, an unexpected shift in awareness literally turned my reality inside out. In a moment that clearly signified the beginning of an impenetrable and rapid spiritual expansion throughout all aspects of my life, it also confirmed the end of struggle, torment, and inner criticism as the radiance of my soul woke up and triumphantly stepped forward.

Whether in the aftermath of tragedy, in response to unavoidable loss, as a remedy for any degree of healing, or in an attempt to satisfy the endless curiosities of our own inner mystery, a modern-day spiritual journey is an opportunity to awaken and explore the light of the soul. One moment of expansion at a time, each fundamental misunderstanding is untangled from the inside out to reveal the radiance of Divine perfection masquerading as life. Meanwhile, every personal encounter offers opportunities for us to evolve into the fullness and uniqueness of our soul's immaculate potential.

While many of us have immersed ourselves in paths of inner growth over the course of many years, there is a profound difference in the degree of relief once we begin to navigate our journey from the soul's perspective. Even after becoming aware of the three activities of ego, it can often feel like such a daunting task to be liberated from the patterns that may have consumed us for so long.

While the conditioned responses of ego may be the source of human suffering, it is meant to be transformed, instead of abandoned or cast away. As we find out throughout each level of a spiritual journey, asserting change from any degree of aggression only fuels the very inner conflicts attempting to be healed. While it is natural to desire life beyond the pitfalls of the ego, a path of transformation requires openness instead of opposition.

From the soul's perspective, the ego's inner WAR can be resolved with the utmost humility. This means approaching our inner evolution with loving-kindness, instead of force or aggression. Since it is inseparable from its wise, harmonious, and omnipresent Source, the soul always resonates with the most loving approach. From this expansive space, we are able to make sense of reality while naturally respecting ourselves, others, and the gravity of our journey as divinity in form.

RESOLUTION MEANS CULTIVATING LIGHT

The ARE equation pinpoints expansion as the effect of combining awareness with resolution. Once we have become aware of the three activities of ego, we are able to learn how to integrate the ego in the most heart-centered way. Instead of spending more time dissecting ourselves under a spiritual microscope, let us explore the fundamental shift that moves us to the forefront of our soul's evolution.

It is more so a change of focus. Instead of always being on alert for more imperfections to fix and change, we open up to cultivating higher frequencies of light. We look at the bigger picture.

In many spiritual circles, the cultivation of light is known as raising our vibration. Instead of battling with inner barriers, which are only enemies for the ego to find, we are honing and refining our most positive qualities. Cultivating light is a willingness to announce the presence of well-being for the benefit of ourselves and those around us.

When our well-being is recognized with greater awareness, we discover the safety and motivation required to put our most empowered qualities on display. No matter how any moment plays out, the ONE in all remains alive in every heart, reminding those who are aware that openness never excludes. We, as Divine stewards of the ONE, have come to this planet on an important mission. We are transforming Earth into its highest potential by announcing the presence of well-being in response to the comings and goings of life.

This may help us realize how the very process that up-lifts the vibration of our energy field is equally the greatest contribution toward shifting the consciousness of an entire civilization. Whether our focus remains singular or global in nature, the very steps required to shift from ego to soul assist in creating a tipping point to awaken the ONE in ALL. If ONE stands for Openness Never Excludes, then ALL is an acronym for Absolute Law (of) Love.

Since Openness Never Excludes is the Absolute Law of Love, it is the cultivation of light that offers us direct and authentic access into experiencing such a cosmic law of inclusion firsthand. The process of cultivating light begins by learning the essential actions that unravel the worry, anticipation, and regret of ego. Whether implemented in response to how often these patterns play out, or merely offering a renewed sense of inspired choices to act upon throughout the day, the spiritual practice of cultivating light is a matter of reversing the acronym of WAR.

FROM WAR TO RAW

When reversing the letters of WAR, the word *RAW* can be seen as its opposite counterpart. As the acronym of RAW is decoded, the natural attributes of our soul are uncovered to allow the spiritual journey to be a communion with Source, instead of a standoff between light and darkness.

The soul already knows that light isn't here to fight with darkness. It has been sent to Earth to rescue darkness from its misery by returning it to the light in the most thoughtful and authentic way. When spirituality is explored by ego, the focus is getting rid of darkness in order to make room for the light. Along a heart-centered path, however, we are no longer caught in a fight with polarity, where good opposes bad or light denies its shadow. Instead, we are learning the way in which the soul naturally behaves in time and space.

As we shift from WAR to RAW, we become announcers of well-being who cultivate light for our soul's expansion. As our vibration elevates, any unconscious pattern, painful memory, or manifestation of darkness is naturally transmuted to complete its mission of returning to Source.

THE BUDDHA DOESN'T FIGHT

One of the clearest demonstrations of shifting from WAR to RAW can be found in the story of the Buddha. As it has been historically depicted, the Buddha while sitting under the Bodhi tree is surrounded by demons. Many see this as the necessity of the Buddha to deny the enticing qualities of ego, or mortal desires, in an attempt to ground firmly into the purity of truth. Of course, having anything to deny could only be a viewpoint of the ego.

Visual depictions of the Buddha show him with his hands resting naturally at each side, with eyes cracked open instead of completely closed. If the Buddha's eyes were shut, the teaching would suggest needing to shun ego or turn away from darkness in order for enlightenment to dawn. Instead, the eyes of the Buddha remain cracked open with arms resting at each side to indicate how the truth is not here to oppose darkness or deny it in any way.

The Buddha is in a state of serenity, even in the presence of demons, because he has realized his true self as the transformer of darkness, the rescuer of ego, the redeemer of light, and the announcer of well-being.

As an evolving spiritual master, by reversing WAR into RAW, you equally will have your own profound moments of enlightenment under the metaphorical Bodhi tree of life. In order to do so, the elements of RAW must be explored.

RAW BEGINS WITH RESPECT

Becoming RAW in its most conscious expression begins with *respect*. The soul's innate quality of respect is a way of honoring the ONE in ALL, whether or not each person in view embodies their divinity honorably.

From the soul's perspective, each scene of interaction was created to offer opportunities for inner growth and spiritual expansion. This places the importance on our personal conduct in response to any circumstance at hand. It means how we respond to ourselves and others becomes far more important to the evolution of our soul than the situations that come to be.

When a desire to remember the ONE in ALL has dawned within us, a tendency to respect each moment and person becomes one of our highest priorities. We can learn to respect the evolution of others, whether or not they understand the gravity of their soul's journey—especially when cruelty and mean-spirited behavior indicates an ego unraveling at a rapid rate.

Equally so, there is *no* spiritual benefit for staying in an environment as someone's mental, emotion, physical, or energetic punching bag. Whether you are called to work things out or leave an abusive situation, the soul is more interested in responding to others with reverence and honor, no matter which decision is meant to be made. Life from the soul's perspective can be seen as a cosmic adventure of "How will I respond?" This can be answered through the deliberate practice of greater respect. For while we may not honor how someone speaks or acts while undergoing the tumultuous effects of inner growth, we can always respect that they have been placed on our path for a very important reason.

As a way of cultivating the vibration of respect, please consider the wisdom of the following questions:

What if I respect the divinity of others, whether or not they acknowledge it in me?

What if I dare to honor my own divinity, instead of waiting for others to see my light?

What if I don't have to respect the unconscious actions of others in order to honor their soul?

What if any moment of disrespect is an opportunity to stop and respect myself at a deeper level?

Are my personal choices demonstrating the deepest respect for myself and others?

If I make it my mission to earn more of my own self-respect on a daily basis, how would my life be different? What would need to change?

With respect leading the way, each opportunity to evolve illuminates the deeper purpose of personal encounters. Whether or not the characters in our reality play the most favorable roles cannot prevent the soul from expanding throughout each scene.

RESPECT IS THE ACTIVITY OF ACKNOWLEDGMENT

When cultivating light by responding with greater respect, we may discover it is nearly impossible to honor life without a willingness to acknowledge it. This is why *acknowledgment* is the second aspect of RAW. Acknowledgment is the very activity of respect that dares to give anything in view the right to be, even when existing in ways that feel painful, frustrating, or inconvenient to the ego.

Even when we are treated disrespectfully by others, this creates an opportunity for us to acknowledge the pain, stress, defensiveness, sadness, and anger as a profound healing taking place. Whether cut off in traffic by those in a rush, criticized by family members, or even betrayed by a loved one, it's amazing to notice how progressive of an expansion occurs in each of our lives, including those who don't even realize they are on a spiritual journey. While it is common to believe that mystical experiences only come to those who are interested in such subject matters, a modern-day spiritual adventure is an opportunity to make sense of the deeply transformative experiences that masquerade as the ups and downs of life. As humans, we are actively participating in the expansion of the soul, even though most of it is spent incubating in ego.

Since awareness is the first component in the equation of ARE, many seekers wish to help those who act disrespectfully to become aware of their unconscious behavior. While it is always important to speak up for ourselves whenever inspired, a necessity for others to acknowledge the shortcomings of their conduct surely gives away our power to their will. When this occurs, we exist in a codependent negotiation with someone else's ego, waiting for them to see the light before our experience can change.

ONLY WE CAN ACKNOWLEDGE

What if anything occurring in reality were only created so we could acknowledge it? What if people only act the way they do to help us become more compassionate, empathetic, and discerning toward others?

When someone acts in a disrespectful way, their soul is attempting to communicate how much pressure they are under as a result of their evolution. This is an expansion that they, as a person, may not even know is happening. Whenever disrespect occurs, their soul is asking for space, so as not to get further distracted from the transformation under way. It's as if any degree of disrespect is an unsuspecting way for their soul to apologize for not being able to show up in the way we may have desired.

Whether we are hurt by a co-worker, friend, neighbor, or loved one, we can acknowledge that disrespectful behavior is how souls request greater physical distance in order to spend more time getting to know themselves beyond the confines of ego.

If someone is meant to interact in a way that is mutually beneficial for the evolution of both souls, their conduct will be open, honest, and respectful. If they are unable to communicate in a respectful manner, their soul is asking for physical space, even if their ego can't stand the thought of being apart.

When someone is more distracted or triggered by our light than soothed and expanded by it, their dishonest or disrespectful behavior will let us know how much space is required. And if this pattern continues on a regular basis, it may be an indication that such a relationship has run its course. When this occurs, the only benefit for either soul to evolve is to move on without the other.

This is a far more empowered way of relating, which replaces the old paradigm approach of orbiting around someone's abusive behavior in an attempt to "accept them as they are." When grounded in our soul's awareness of acknowledgment, others are able to benefit from our vibration when they are able to act respectfully. If there are insights and answers within us that are pivotal to their journey, they will ask questions that inspire such wisdom as a way of letting us know the exact gift we can provide.

If they don't ask questions that inspire our deepest wisdom, it is their soul's way of letting us know that while we have much to share, they may not be ready or have the mental space to take in new ideas, concepts, or perspectives.

While you may be nearly jumping out of your skin, wanting to offer a morsel of truth that can uplift the nature of someone else's experiences, such transformation is only ready to be received when others are open to greater insights through the questions they are willing to ask.

No matter how openhearted or closed-minded anyone seems to be, we can still assist in the evolution of their journey. This occurs by choosing to be a source of emotional comfort as the ups and downs of life run their course. From this space, we come to realize how in most instances people need greater emotional support and personal encouragement, rather than more information to process. In the old paradigm, it is believed that we can help ourselves and others more by doing more. In the new spiritual paradigm, we lead with respect, while grounded in the simplicity of acknowledgment. We remain open to the signs others offer to hold conscious space for their healing without needing to overextend ourselves or overstay our welcome.

To help activate the power of acknowledgment, please consider the wisdom of the following questions:

Am I assuming the needs of myself and others, or am I acknowledging the signs that are offered?

Can I acknowledge my own need for personal space whenever I respond with disrespect?

Am I willing to offer space to others when they disrespect me?

What am I willing to acknowledge right now that has gone overlooked or avoided throughout my life?

Are there any choices I am making that disrespect the integrity of myself or others?

Through the power of acknowledgment, each sign the Universe sends your way can be decoded with peace, ease, and joy. As the second attribute of the soul is embraced on a regular basis, the cruelty and heartless nature of other people's actions become instrumental feedback in knowing how to navigate the terrain of our journey.

ALL IS WELCOMED

The Absolute Law of Love is that Openness Never Excludes. As suggested by the acronym ALL ONE, everything can be honored as a creation of Source when viewing life from the soul's perspective. While some believe the offering of personal space to those who act disrespectfully conveys a form of rejection or exclusion, it is paramount to always stand tall in the heart-centered truth of our Divine essence.

This means we are able to celebrate the light in all, while also discerning when our presence is or isn't the best offering for the evolution of another. To provide the boundary of personal space on a temporary or permanent basis is only a form of rejection for an ego that feeds off the validation of specific characters. Personal space may not be the gift we or someone else desires, but it may be the exact medicine either soul needs for the deepest inner growth. This can be true for partnerships, friendships, or even bonds with family members: Recognizing the need for space as a gift of solitude instead of a curse of rejection may liberate both souls into the direction of their highest destiny.

This is why the ability to *welcome* life on its precise terms and conditions is the third aspect of RAW. As a way of offering greater focus to the soul's perspective, we welcome the actions of life with reverence and honesty.

When we lead with the attribute of welcoming, we honor each creation as an expression of Source, knowing each person exists on their own unique journey through time and space. When we exist in an active state of welcoming, we are aware that others are placed in our reality for the evolution of our soul, whether or not they play the roles we desire.

No matter how much or how little someone else can meet you in the same open space you offer, by moving forward with a welcoming perspective you invite the gifts of each moment to be acknowledged with greater heartfelt respect.

To inspire the attribute of welcoming, please consider the wisdom of the following questions:

Can I welcome life openly no matter how it seems or appears?

Am I aware of the spiritual benefits that each encounter offers, even when it hurts, inconveniences, or frustrates my ego?

How does my experience of thoughts, feelings, the world, and others change when I choose to welcome it?

What newly empowered choices am I willing to welcome into my life for the evolution of my soul?

Simply by welcoming each moment, we are inviting the evolutionary benefits of each encounter to help end the inner WAR. A war is defined as an invasion or as a conflict between two opposing sides. If any side is welcomed versus opposed, then there exists no conflict to resolve.

UNRAVELING WAR WITH RAW

Instead of spending time hiding under a spiritual microscope of self-judgment and inner criticism, our soul's journey is centered in cultivating higher vibrations of light. This occurs by transforming the way we respond to ourselves and others. In doing so, we soften the edges of ego to help it return to Source.

Again, this is not a matter of casting ego away, but rather realizing the Source that ego is meant to find is the spark of divinity within you. One inspired moment at a time, the inner WAR is unraveled by daring to be RAW in the most authentic, compassionate, and heart-centered way.

From this space, the Absolute Law of Love reveals the truth of our Infinite Source, as that which Welcomes Each Life as Light.

Absolute Law (of) Love = ALL

Infinite Source = IS

Welcomes Each Life (as) Light = WELL

ALL IS WELL.

**To help embody the insight of ALL IS WELL,
please consider the wisdom of or repeat
aloud the following statement:**

I accept that my spiritual journey is not a matter of dissecting myself under a spiritual microscope but allowing my soul's highest innate qualities to shine through more consistently and deliberately. This occurs by respecting the divinity in others, acknowledging the signs offered to best support each person's unique journey of healing, and welcoming the circumstances that inspire my most profound expansion, whether it matches my desires or not.

In knowing it is so, I allow all RAW qualities of the soul's highest attributes to be activated within and to radiate throughout for the well-being of all. From this moment forward, I am naturally rooted in the enthusiasm of each gift I am here to offer. I don't have to be afraid of what others may take from me or withhold from my heart. There is a reason I am here. I exist with purpose. I came here to matter. And so it is.

As we embrace the RAW qualities of our soul's highest attributes, we begin to see how everything is here to help us grow, expand, and evolve, even when initially appearing as obstacles in our path.

CHAPTER 3

HOW
EVERYTHING
HELPS

AS WE COME TO KNOW **ALL IS WELL** as a naturally lived experience, it becomes more instinctive for each perceivable enemy or obstacle to be respected, acknowledged, and welcomed as an ally in disguise. While the ego remains capable of embracing only the people, places, and things that fulfill its desires, the soul sees reality from a viewpoint beyond the comparisons of pain and pleasure. Because ego is the soul in its most dormant stages of evolution, it is conditioned to respond unconsciously to reality through judgments of polarity. This means the ego is attracted to one thing as a way of avoiding another.

For example, the ego often desires the thrill of winning as a successful avoidance of losing. It can yearn for the pleasure of relationship to avoid the pain of loneliness. Maybe it seeks more personal gains to fill the void inspired by loss. Perhaps it wishes for greater health merely as a way of averting potential

illness or even seeking out spiritual practices or healing modalities to chase each concern away.

It is natural for pain to be the least likely experience we
would prefer to have, but when grounded in the brightness
of our soul, it can be acknowledged as evidence of spiritual
evolution. This doesn't mean we must always be in pain in
order to grow, nor do we have to imagine pain as a barrier
to our deepest pleasure. When any moment of discomfort
arises, by responding in a more heart-centered manner it becomes a powerful opportunity to cultivate higher frequencies
of light. Focusing on how honorably and lovingly we respond
to any experience, we allow ourselves to view life from the
soul's perspective.

THE NATURE OF ADVERSITY

As a way of revealing the spiritual ally that resides in the appearance of each enemy, obstacle, or barrier, it is important
to understand the purpose of adversity and its role in our
journey.

While adversity seems to be a universal rite of passage
along the road of life, it can be a nearly intangible concept
to grasp, simply because any form of adversity is dependent
on the viewpoint of the experiencer. What may seem cruel
and intolerable to one person may be a passing experience of
unexpected circumstances to another, depending upon how
rooted in WAR or aligned in RAW one tends to be.

No matter how painful a circumstance, and regardless of
whether it causes us to fight, flee, or freeze, adversity is an
interpretation of the ego created in response to unexpected
changes in inner or outer environments. While the ego is capable of embracing the changes that meet its every demand,
it is not equipped with the coping skills and practical wisdom

to view each outcome from an expanded perspective. Unlike the ego, the soul is able to stay true to its experience. It naturally recognizes the evolutionary gifts that arrive, often wrapped in the most unexpected packages.

To the soul, unexpected or undesirable changes can occur without igniting the heat of inner conflict. This is because the soul understands the nature of evolution through the laws of alchemy. Just as solid objects can be melted into liquid or vaporous states through applications of heat, one of the most efficient ways of transforming ego into soul is by surviving the fire of adversity.

Since the gifts of adversity through each stage of our journey exclusively benefit the consciousness within us, only the soul can embrace such a process. As the light of divinity expands and grounds into our body, we reach such a transcendent state of reality that evolution can take place without requiring the fire of adversity to continue to burn. As incredible as it may sound, when rooted in the brightness of the soul, greater spiritual growth can occur without requiring pain, stress, or adversity to play such key roles. And yet, for so many lifetimes, the ego has been trying to harness the power of the Universe through various mystical pathways in an attempt to avoid the encounters that inspire more unraveling.

This means a spiritual journey is not about making our egos more educated or powerful, but about aligning with the soul, so it can be integrated once and for all. Whether you know why or how, everything is here to help you transition from ego to soul. This insight helps transform reality, from dense perceptions of solid matter into the vastness of light that initially requires the heat of adversity to inspire a proper melting point.

Even when it seems like the characters throughout our lives are conspiring against us, it is the grace of the Universe, personified as the actions of each person, which creates the exact circumstances, outcomes, and environments to ensure our most triumphant victory.

Ultimately, it is our willingness to honor, acknowledge, and welcome the mystery of each moment that allows expansion to unfold with ease. No matter how deeply we wish our circumstances were different, a time-honored shift from ego to soul occurs by discovering the ally residing in each enemy. Even if you are unaware of the gifts that come to be, by embracing the wisdom that *everything* is here to help you, the destiny of your RAW potential can be discovered—without finding more worry, anticipation, or regret to resolve.

ENEMIES AS SPIRITUAL ALLIES

When adversity arises, the conditioned rhythm of our unconscious patterning is interrupted. This is why adversity could only be seen as an enemy to the ego; the ego cannot survive outside the domain of incubation. But, in fact, every perceivable enemy is a spiritual ally in disguise.

Exploring reality outside the climate of human conditioning is much like adjusting to life at a higher altitude. Just as the body requires time and care to learn how to breathe when the air feels thin, our consciousness goes through a similar period of adjustment as we learn to live from higher dimensions of perception.

As unconscious patterns are interrupted, we are offered space from the ego as a way of adjusting to a more expanded spiritual standpoint. But the unexpected changes of stress, conflict, or adversity often elicit responses of fear at first, because most of our lives have been spent viewing life from the perspective of ego. It can be shocking, confusing, and even intimidating when the nature of unexpected change thrusts us into experiences outside of our known beliefs or reference points. When comforted by our most familiar patterns of conditioning, the inevitability of change can quickly become an enemy to avoid. And yet, as we open up to life beyond a struggle between pleasure and pain, we can get to know the beauty of life outside the domain of ego, no matter how frustrating, inconvenient, shocking, or painful each adversity seems to be.

In order to truly embrace how everything is here to help you, it is important to examine such a truth throughout our deepest moments of discomfort.

THE GIFT OF LOSS

While loss is often perceived by the ego as scenarios of impending doom, the inevitability of change could only take away from life the very things that create space for something new to emerge. No matter how much time there seems to be in between losses and gains, the purpose of loss is to strip the ego of any false sense of power, in order to help it unravel. While the ego insists on having the ability to return to the light willingly, it would only do so under such specific terms and conditions that it would keep itself completely intact.

Since the light of Source energy is empty or formless in nature, the ego must be dissolved out of its defined structure so it can merge back into Source as vibration, instead of form.

This means the unraveling of ego cannot occur when and how the ego would prefer it. Instead, it is the spontaneous moments of unexpected change or loss that signify a readiness for spiritual expansion. We certainly don't have to like how it feels when the things that define our sense of worth, purpose, or safety dissolve out of sight. And yet loss and change can be honored as spiritual rites of passage, instead of unwarranted moments of cruel misfortune.

A REASON FOR FEAR

Even something as debilitating as fear is here to help you. While it is common to perceive fear as a prime roadblock to liberation, there is a deeper purpose for why it exists. Fear acts as an aspect of intuition, though it is reduced into states of compulsive worry when we are incubating in ego. Just as many people receive gut instincts that intrinsically guide them away from danger, fear is often a sign of preparation. It acts as a reminder to inform us when unexpected moments of greater expansion are set to occur.

During moments of fear, a signal is sent from the Universe. It lets the ego know that whatever situation has produced such a frightful feeling is a moment in time, where the ego will further unravel by facing some degree of frustration, inconvenience, loss, or change.

Because each moment of our journey occurs in a space of free will, we always have the right to say: *Thank you, Universe, for the signal of fear, in response to whatever choice or situation is being considered. I understand that instead of everything going my way, from start to finish, fear is letting me know that I may be facing inconveniences, frustrations, or threats of unexpected loss and change as part of my evolution. I will take some time to consider whether I am up for such a spontaneous moment of growth, knowing that if I choose to pass on this fearful choice, it will be revisited and faced at a later date. Thank you, Universe, for this opportunity to communicate and cooperate together.*

Even though the inevitability of inconvenience, frustration, loss, and change serves to unravel ego, when viewing fear as an aspect of intuition, we can make more empowered decisions, whether or not we know how anything is meant to unfold.

There may be some days when we welcome the personal challenges that signify the expansion of our soul with confidence and enthusiasm. There may also be times when we're not as excited to celebrate the learning of another life lesson and wish to have some space to coast along. If the expansion of the soul is our cosmic job, then deciding not to venture in the direction of fear is like calling into the office and taking a personal day off. We may not be able to avoid the grace of change forever, but we certainly can learn to work with the Universe to ensure our evolution unfolds in the most supportive way.

THE WISDOM OF ANGER

Since many past traumas are inspired by the unconscious expression of anger, it is natural to shut down when such an emotion is triggered. Whether it is fear of the retribution of others or of the harm we may project outward, anger exists as one of our fiercest allies when recognized, acknowledged, and welcomed as a helper in disguise.

From the standpoint of ego, anger is a reaction to being wronged or rejected. Because ego exists in an unconscious state of incubation, it perceives rejection or wrongdoing whenever it doesn't get its way. As our consciousness expands, we become keenly aware that even when outcomes don't seem to align with our deepest desires—it doesn't necessarily indicate any injustice has occurred.

From the perspective of the soul, no character needs to be blamed for the outcomes in play or even for the emotions that get triggered. Since the deepest aspiration of the soul is to respond from its highest consciousness, no matter how unfair situations seem to be, it is essential to make peace with anger so it can serve us as the ally it was created to be.

When anger is an ally, it acts as a guardian of our energy field. Just as fear is a way for the Universe to prepare us for impending moments of unraveling, anger acts as the protector of our innocent nature. It steps forward like a courageous guard whenever the circumstances that inspire our most profound expansion become too overwhelming to process. Since disrespect is the activity of anger in its most unconscious form, anger also offers vital insights into our experiences with others.

Whether we are treated disrespectfully or feel surges of personal fury, the wisdom of anger reminds us when greater space is necessary for the expansions taking place.

No matter how much benefit we believe can be offered to others, when anger is present, the guardian of their energy field is offering vital feedback. This means the exact gift of space that anger may invite us to offer another is equally the same gift we are urged to receive for the transformation of our journey.

When rooted in ego, it is common to relate to others on the basis of a search for constant personal validation, instead of engaging in the dance of true emotional intimacy that only the soul can navigate. Based on the patterns of human conditioning, personal interactions are often pursued to fill up spaces of emotional deficiency—only to create greater hunger and desperation along the way.

When relationships are created from ego, they're more likely to be entanglements of codependency and victimhood than meaningful bonds and intimate partnerships. In a codependent relationship, it is common to focus more on the things we desire from others than to recognize the gifts each of us have brought to mutually receive *together.*

As we shift from ego to soul, anger becomes an ally of awareness to help transform each relationship into the highest vibration of everlasting fulfillment. While no relationship can be guaranteed to last forever, we are able to be endeared by the gifts that fill each partnership, no matter how long-term or short-lived each connection is meant to be.

With anger as an ally, we are able to know when the gift of space is necessary, whether for ourselves or others. When the wisdom of anger is acknowledged, we are able to recognize someone's insensitive response, disrespectful behavior, or defensiveness as a sign that they are processing an expansion that has overwhelmed their innocence.

While an ego will insist on rescuing someone from their experiences, the soul offers space for someone to process their feelings and remains open to engagement, once an invitation has been offered.

Whether in response to global events or in the presence of a heated argument, the wisdom of anger reminds us when our innocence is far too overwhelmed by the depths of spiritual evolution to have the capacity to consciously engage. If we are relating to an ego, we are likely to be backed into a metaphorical corner and pressed for answers with no regard for the well-being of our experience. When engaging with the soul, any degree of differences can be discussed with openness and authenticity. If anger arises in either heart, the conversation can be paused, so each can tend to their personal feelings and, once the anger passes, return to the discussion.

In essence, people, places, and things don't make us angry. Our anger is due to the space we don't know how to provide, when relationships focus more on the things we can get from others rather than the beauty of sharing ourselves with those we love.

HOW JUDGMENT CAN HELP

What if we thought of judgment as another form of intuition?

From the perspective of ego, judgments are the criticisms that divide our hearts from those that seem foreign to our known perceptions of reality. When incubating in ego, judgments are mental or verbal attacks against the threat of change, whether arising as slander, racism, stereotyping, gender objectification, or ridiculing the lifestyle of another.

The destiny of the ego is to unravel, therefore it lives in such a fragile state that being in the presence of someone who thinks, acts, speaks, or looks differently has the potential to inspire a whirlwind of defensiveness. When rooted in the brightness of the soul, all beings are inherently honored as unique expressions of our one eternal Source. No matter how different someone seems, there is a natural acceptance that each person is guided along their own path to engage the experiences that are useful for their growth. While the soul is naturally welcoming of the very changes that ego fights at every turn, the soul still has a journey of profound growth. One such example is recognizing the appearance of any judgment as an intuition being received.

If everything is here to help you, then even judgment must contain some degree of usefulness. Even when packaged in the appearance of a harsh criticism toward ourselves or others, by learning how to decode each intuitive message, a life of insufferable pain becomes a journey of majestic revelation.

The soul is so sensitive to other people's experiences that it often misunderstands its empathic abilities as personal judgments. When fully realized, the pitfalls of ego reveal the greater healing power of an awakening soul.

Here's a perfect example: I remember standing in line at the grocery store many years ago where the person in front of me was of a different ethnicity. As I stood behind him, I began hearing in my head the most outrageously disrespectful words and phrases. For a split second, I thought my mind had become spontaneously racist!

This alarmed me since I grew up as someone who defended others against bullies and always stood up for kids who were being discriminated against for their ethnic background. Historically speaking, I despised any kind of insults, no matter how quickly the kids who were called out for their actions claimed they were joking.

Anytime a kid came to my school from a different country, I became a one-boy welcoming committee. I grew up with a wide range of friends of many ethnic backgrounds and loved getting to know cultures that seemed so different from how I was raised. So you can imagine how confusing it was to hear such words in my head, even though I didn't consciously identify with any of them. As this unfolded, I began feeling layers of discrimination unraveling out of the energy field. This person in the grocery store may not necessarily be open to any type of healing—which is perhaps the reason why the Universe placed me in his view. As I felt each layer unravel, I was relieved to know that each racist thought was not something I was thinking. I was becoming aware of the ancestral imprints that my energy field was clearing out.

When there is any degree of incubation occurring in our energy field, the thoughts we have and the feelings we notice are often translated as judgments toward ourselves or others. As incubation dissolves, the brightness of the soul realizes its true potency and power, as a healer, awakener, and transformer of reality. While such healing may traditionally take place in the office of a practitioner, the majority of deep healing work spontaneously occurs throughout each personal interaction.

Instead of judging each thought as if we came up with it, why not be open to the possibility that each limiting idea, belief, or thought is a layer of the collective unconscious that we are healing for the well-being of all?

Within the old spiritual paradigm, it can be quite confusing to experience such negative thinking, especially if we believe our thoughts have any influence over the outcomes of reality.

Consider the possibility that thoughts do not create reality, since all of reality already exists. When we were born, we did not wait for reality to appear. We were welcomed into a world that was already created, simply waiting for us to arrive. While there are a multiplicity of options to choose from, thoughts do not determine what does or does not happen.

This is because outcomes unfolding as destiny are created prior to each human incarnation. While thoughts can determine the quality of experience, whether from the viewpoint of the ego or the perspective of the soul, we don't have to project judgments or superstitions onto experiences that merely confirm the emotional debris our energy fields are clearing out of those in view.

Even when we feel as if we are judging someone, a much deeper experience is likely happening: Primarily, the judgments we hear are the insults they have had projected onto them by others or have concluded about themselves. Here we are, as lightworkers in human form, clearing emotional layers out of their field, simply by standing in their presence. Even when such judgments contain a feeling of aversion or disgust toward someone, it is the wisdom of the soul sending an important message. Since we tend to match the vibration of those we spend the most time with, feelings of aversion are a way for inner guidance to remind us when we are choosing to spend time with someone whose energy may exhaust us instead of uplift us.

This can be quite confusing for an evolving, energetically sensitive soul who always yearns to assist in the healing of others and support the underdog in any story. Through the eyes of the Universe, those we are meant to heal have us feeling uplifted instead of exhausted. And when feelings that were once uplifting suddenly create a sense of exhaustion, that is the Universe suggesting that we have shared enough space with that person for the time being. Instead of attempting to push past this energetic boundary, the Universe reminds us how we would be better suited to rest and integrate the exchange that has occurred.

Just as we are clearing the energy fields of others, the energy fields of others are doing the same for us. While healings auspiciously take place from one moment to the next, the energy being cleared out tends to linger in the field of each healer when perceived from the viewpoint of ego.

As we begin viewing life from the soul's perspective, we come to understand our inherent healing abilities that shed the layers of emotional debris that are ready to be released. Just by knowing such healing is happening, there can be less self-judgment projected onto our feelings. This allows the debris we are clearing to return to Source instead of being added to our conditioning. When we are asleep in ego, we unknowingly take on other people's energy. But when we are rooted in the soul, we are feeling the layers of emotion that our energy fields are clearing out of those around us.

THE BENEFIT OF OVERTHINKING

Just as the ego can be honored as the soul in its most dormant stages of expansion, the mind is not an enemy to oppose but an ally to embrace. While the experience of an overthinking mind can be quite distracting and frustrating to encounter, there is always a greater purpose for why it occurs. No matter how noisy or relentless it seems, even the overthinking mind is here to help you.

The activity of mind reflects how open or closed our heart tends to be.

The more our heart is permitted to open, the easier it is for ego to unravel. We can think of the overactive mind as an alarm clock. Whenever our heart is shutting down, either from being overwhelmed by the depth of expansion occurring in our field or due to the amount of debris we are unknowingly clearing out of others, our mind informs us by becoming noisy.

Once we realize a noisy mind is not a spiritual barrier to resolve, but rather a clever tool of transformation for our evolutionary benefit, we are able to make peace with any degree of overthinking.

As this occurs, our relationship with mind becomes more respectful in nature, allowing the heart to remain more naturally open.

It's ironic to realize that once we acknowledge the deeper purpose of a noisy mind, it assists us in becoming so heart-centered that no such alarm may be needed.

Whether embroiled in victimhood or unknowingly lightening the load of other people's energy fields, the activity of mind demonstrates whether we are viewing reality from a conscious or unconscious standpoint. By honoring the deeper purpose of overthinking, we assist in absolving the mind of playing such a role in our lives.

From this space, we become so grounded in heart-centered consciousness that we are able to uplift the vibration of others, instead of lowering our energy to relate with the hardships of their perceptions.

A DEEPER PURPOSE FOR SADNESS

Sadness confirms the exact moments in time when the ego dissolves. While it is possible for the ego to unravel in one profound moment of transcendence, it is far more common for it to dissolve back into Source in a more gradual way. Sadness is the ego's response when life fails to fulfill its insatiable list of demands and desires. Whenever the ego doesn't get its way, it either lashes out in anger or shuts down in sadness. And since the ego isn't capable of recognizing how each defense could only be in response to the expansion of the soul, it firmly believes everything it feels is due to not having its needs met.

In reality, any outcome that inspires sadness is only playing out in precise fashion to create more room for the soul to shine through. In essence, outcomes of any kind don't cause us to feel any particular way. Instead, we are feeling exactly how we feel in direct response to our soul's expansion. Additionally, once we realize the feelings that signify the soul's expansion equally represent the patterns our energy fields are purging out of others, it becomes easier to allow feelings to move through us as they return to Source.

When we're rooted in ego, believing these experiences are the reason we feel the way we do, sadness maintains an insufferable grip. Yet, as we transition from ego to soul, situations are created merely to make us aware of the feelings that are equally being cleared out of our fields as well as those of others. This allows the emotion of sadness to take on a transitory quality.

When this occurs, our emotions confirm vital milestones of expansion, instead of perpetuating our beliefs in victimhood.

Usually, sadness only orbits our experiences in recurring fashion or spends so much time in our reality when we view it as a *barrier* we need to overcome. Again, the ego could never go along with the evolutionary benefits that sadness provides, simply because it would keep the ego from unraveling. While ego is unaware that dissolving back into Source remains its true life purpose, no amount of effort or negotiating can prevent this from taking place. To the best of its ability, the ego may try to be at the forefront of personal growth, but true growth can only be discovered as the ego is dissolved.

And while the ego cannot help this process, it certainly cannot hinder it, either. This is precisely why a spiritual journey in the new paradigm offers the most loving way of shifting from ego to soul. It can be quite depressing to experience the fate of our highest evolution from the viewpoint of a dissolving ego; on the other hand, it can be quite elating and joyful to explore our path when grounded in the purity of the soul.

When rooted in the brightness of the soul, sadness does not represent a deficiency of happiness. Sadness is merely how the heart adjusts to loss and releases patterns of attachment for the well-being of all. Every time sadness arises, the body has an emotional garage sale; it releases whatever is no longer needed for the journey ahead and clears space to welcome in what our entire lives have prepared us to find—true happiness. In order for our evolution to feel far less depressing and much more exciting, we want to respect, acknowledge, and welcome our experiences, no matter how sad they seem to be.

AN UPSIDE TO DISAPPOINTMENT

When viewing life through the lens of ego, disappointment is the death of expectation with no awareness of its evolutionary benefits. From the soul's perspective, however, the role of disappointment is to liberate our consciousness from the dream of expectation, so we can remain open to the fate of life's infinite possibilities.

In many cases, the ego believes the best-case scenario is getting exactly what it wants. From this point of view, many attachments to outcome are created, and life only has one way to make us happy: future pending desires of long-lasting pleasure. As we shift from ego to soul, we are open to the *endless* ways we can experience true happiness, without always needing to get our way in order for life to seem fair.

As disappointment arises, the death of expectation expands awareness beyond the limitations of self-defeating beliefs and attachments to outcomes. When disappointed, the ego feels the sting of personal defeat, as the inevitable waves of sadness signify deeper layers of ego being released—both in ourselves and others. This is precisely why the ego cannot ever attain the goals set forth on a spiritual journey. If the ego were to achieve each milestone, it would be getting its way.

Since the emergence of the soul occurs in the ego's dissolution, it is the perpetual tendency of ego not getting its way that allows disappointment to assist in the process.

We certainly don't have to enjoy how it feels when disappointment arises, and it cannot be something we anticipate. Oftentimes, when we least expect it, the death of expectation arrives at the doorstep of reality to remove more distractions from our path, instead of feeding the aspect of self that only grows hungry for more. The question remains, are we ready to embrace how even disappointment is here to help us, or will we maintain the inner WAR by withholding our highest Divine attributes until life fulfills each expectation?

THE PROPHETIC POWER OF JEALOUSY

One of the most polarizing and isolating emotions is jealousy. From the viewpoint of ego, jealousy is a fury of injustice when viewing the things we most desire as they appear in other people's lives. Jealousy really acts as a foreshadowing of all the blessings that are *destined* to be received. In most cases, the signs of incoming blessings take on a broader confirmation.

Through the eyes of the Universe, physical reality represents emotional states as tangible matter. Essentially, we only truly desire the things we want because of how we imagine we would feel if such things were given. This means the objects of our desire are not actually objects that we desire. What is truly desired, beyond attachments to any particular outcome, is to feel the wide array of positive emotions that confirm our complete alignment with Source energy.

While it is possible that someone else's job promotion, brand-new relationship, or windfall of opportunity foreshadows the exact gifts the Universe is sending our way, it more likely reveals more about the feelings we desire. Since optimal feelings are not dependent upon specific outcomes and circumstances, the amplified blessings of others signify a readiness to feel more in the way we truly desire, which occurs through the expansion of the soul.

While the ego remains mesmerized by the objects it seeks, it exists as a conditioned view of dormant consciousness, destined only to chase each craving while never finding true fulfillment, no matter how many blessings it receives. This reveals discontent as the natural state of the ego. As long as we exist in some degree of incubation, discontent recurs, despite the arrangement of personal circumstance.

And yet, funnily enough, any amount of time spent in discontent tends to build momentum for greater expansion.

Since everything is here to help you, jealousy is like a message sent from the Universe reminding you of all the blessings that are on their way into your reality. Whether or not they take shape and form as the features and benefits present in other people's lives, jealousies ensure an expansion of well-being as we step further into the ecstasy of our highest evolution.

Although many people tend to judge themselves for feeling jealous, it is simply a matter of how we respond to the feeling that determines our level of consciousness. If the ego has adopted a spiritual identity, it will insist on being beyond such lower vibrational emotions. While a fully embodied soul may not experience emotions such as jealousy on a regular basis, the truth of heart-centered consciousness is so deeply humbled by the auspicious reverence of life that no feeling is denied, condemned, or compared against another.

Like every other experience, jealousy could only be here to help you, whether you're feeling the jealousy you're clearing out of others, swirling in discontent in preparation for greater expansion, or recognizing the sneak previews of greater blessings on their way.

AN UNEXPECTED LIBERATOR

Resentment is the residue of blame. It is an unconscious tendency to judge and blame the people in our lives for the expansion each outcome inevitably inspires. No matter how unsavory these characters are, resentment is a subtle form of jealousy toward those who demonstrate more freedom of will than we allow ourselves to express. Such people may not use their free will in the most conscious, productive, or compassionate way, and may even demonstrate their freedom through abusive tendencies. And yet, when we can recognize our resentment as reminders of how often we hold back from expressing our greatest potential in form, each moment of finger-pointing can be utilized for an evolutionary benefit.

Energetically sensitive beings are naturally heart-centered, and they often do not unleash their freedom of will in ways that those who incubate in ego tend to do. This is often why it is so easy to get hurt, angered, heartbroken, or disappointed by the actions of those who are only out for themselves.

No matter how often we seem to attract the mindless behavior of other people throughout our lives, they have been placed along our path for two specific reasons. The first reason is the innate healing power of our energy field to help lighten their load, which occurs by the feelings we sense as a result of each encounter. The ego may not like the idea of attracting experiences of victimhood as a way of uplifting the vibration of those around us—though the more you transition from ego to soul, the easier it is to heal others without getting entangled.

The second reason we may attract the cruelty of others is to challenge and eventually dissolve any limiting beliefs that prevent us from noticing the light of divinity in all. Just as seeds must dissolve in order for flowers to blossom, the characters in our reality need to express their Source energy at various levels of growth and maturity.

And yet from the viewpoint of ego, it is nearly instinctive to look past the eternal truth of another when they fail to demonstrate their soul's highest qualities.

For the ego, resentment is the residue of blaming others for the conditions we notice; for the soul, resentment is an unexpected liberator, creating more space for compassion to grow. Compassion is our innate ability to notice each condition and admit the honesty of our experience, even taking swift, courageous action when necessary, while forgiving each character along the way.

THE SOUND OF CONFLICT

Many people develop an aversion to uncomfortable emotions, not just based on how painful they feel but also because they tend to be unclear on how to experience such feelings consciously. Since many outdated approaches view lower vibrational emotions in a superstitious way, it causes many to feel like spiritual failures for expressing the human side of their divinity.

When a seeker has transformed their conditioning into a spiritual ego, there can be a deep-rooted sense of guilt or shame when they feel frustrated, out of the flow, or triggered by the unconsciousness of others.

In order to unravel each aspect of ego without adopting a more spiritually decorated persona, it is essential to learn how to experience reality in the most heart-centered way.

The more consciously we experience the terms and conditions of conflicts, the more we benefit spiritually. This doesn't mean we have to pretend to like experiences that cause pain. It is simply a matter of understanding the difference between reacting from ego versus responding as the soul.

The difference between how our ego reacts and how the soul responds can often be a matter of sound. The fact that inner and outer worlds seem to be two different realities is for our evolutionary benefit. Whether we are noticing thoughts or feelings from the viewpoint of ego or from the soul's perspective, each and every time it is an empathic result of raising the vibration of the collective unconscious.

As expressions of Source in form, we have incarnated into this earthly realm as a vivid course of angelic study. Each of us, no matter how we act or appear, expresses the uniqueness of our light through a journey of expansion. Additionally, we are learning about the soul's most profound healing abilities as it furthers the journeys of those we meet.

Whether we are able to release out of our fields the debris cleared from others or merely are adding it to the conditioning orbiting within us, it is often a matter of how much or how little sound we make that determines the vibration of our experience.

When incubating in ego, uncomfortable internal experiences elicit external noise. When someone is unconsciously processing anger in their energy field, they tend to sound aggressive or speak loudly. The ego cannot abide in silence when any degree of emotional healing takes place.

Whether it begins as a passive-aggressive muttering to oneself about the unfairness of a situation or escalates into a shouting match between two people, the amount of noise that is outwardly expressed is often a sign of unconscious experiences. The more unconscious it is, the more likely one is taking on the energy cleared out of others, instead of allowing each emotion to pass through and integrate back into Source.

Of course, there are times when in order to process and release the energies being cleared, it is essential to put words to our experiences and even share them with those in our lives. The question is: Are we sharing from an open space of peaceful authenticity, or are we projecting our feelings onto people we insist must meet our demands?

Many spiritual egos interpret "speaking the truth" as an open invitation to cast blame and pass judgment onto others who act out in a way that confirms their most limiting beliefs. On the other hand, the soul is able to share its feelings without any degree of yelling or finger-pointing. From the ego's standpoint, no amount of healing occurs unless those we engage with agree with our perspective. This is why arguments can only occur in the domain of ego, since it is the conditioned self that only knows how to share through the sounds of conflict.

This doesn't mean that all outbursts of laughter are indications of ego consciousness; it depends on the *tone*. If the tone is mean-spirited or sarcastic, then we see how that person's words and actions demonstrate the unconsciousness at play.

THE POWER OF THE BREATH

Instead of trying to respect, acknowledge, and welcome our experiences as a consecutive process, what if there were a way to cultivate the qualities of RAW all at once? This is possible by recognizing one of the soul's most powerful tools of transformation.

It is the power of the *breath*.

When we choose to breathe through circumstance, instead of arguing about it, we are respecting, acknowledging, and welcoming the evolutionary benefits of an encounter all at once. Since arguments are outward expressions of shallow breathing, our willingness to meet internal emotional chaos with the sustenance of conscious breath allows the soul to expand.

When we are able to feel instead of blame, and breathe instead of argue, we are stepping to the forefront of our highest angelic potential as evolving spiritual masters. Whether or not someone acts in a way that deserves our respect, acknowledgment, or warmest welcome, the brightness of the soul is always ready to respond more consciously than any character in view.

Until this shift into the soul's perspective dawns, the unavoidable change ebbing and flowing throughout our reality will continue to trigger the inner WAR of ego. This painful odyssey, however, comes to an end the moment we recognize how anything that appears as an enemy is a spiritual ally helping us grow. This insight is not something to blindly believe but an expanded view of reality that must be breathed into our essence, in order to reveal the magnificent truth the soul already knows.

To help embody the insights of this chapter, please consider the wisdom of or repeat aloud the following statement:

I accept that everything I experience is only here to help me. Whether representing patterns of emotional debris clearing out of my field or acknowledged as layers of unconsciousness healed throughout the collective, I honor each thought and feeling for its highest evolutionary benefit: I embrace the nature of adversity that helps to create a proper melting point to transform personal rigidity into the light of my original form. I honor the gift of loss as it clears space in my reality for greater gifts to emerge. I acknowledge a deeper reason for fear as signals from the Universe of impending moments of growth.

I respect the wisdom of anger that reveals when someone is too overwhelmed by their healing journey to be able to interact in a heart-centered way. I welcome judgment as a helper who reminds me of the limiting beliefs I am clearing out of my energy field as well as that of others. I embrace the benefit of overthinking as an alarm clock informing me how open or closed my heart tends to be.

I recognize a deeper purpose for sadness, as it arises in the very moments when the ego dissolves. I realize there is an upside to disappointment, as the ego is given further permission to unravel whenever it doesn't get its way. I recognize the prophetic power of jealousy as a foreshadowing of greater blessings entering my reality, whether or not it matches the exact gifts others are destined to receive. I appreciate resentment as an unexpected liberator that shows me the areas of my life where I hold back from expressing my freedom of will at full capacity.

Instead of getting tangled up in the sounds of conflict, I can respect, honor, and welcome each spiritual ally for its highest evolutionary benefit through the power of my breath. In doing so, I serve my purpose as an angel in human form who incarnated to uplift the collective without having to dim my light or match the vibration of those around me. And so I am free.

As each spiritual ally is embraced for its precise evolutionary benefit, we allow a deeper wellspring of peace to guide us into greater harmony with the mystery of life, not needing to always know where life is headed in order to become who we were always destined to be.

CHAPTER 4

BALANCING
THE MASCULINE
AND THE
FEMININE

AS WE BECOME MORE ALIGNED with breath to transform our inner WAR into the RAW attributes of the soul's reality, many seemingly opposing forces come into more harmonious order.

Just as every creation maintains a sense of alignment through relationships of interdependence, in every human being there are both masculine and feminine energies to be balanced. While we may be depicted as a character of a specific gender, the masculine and feminine energies represent two sides of the whole human experience. In order to discover the necessary balance between these two forces, it is important to explore masculine and feminine energies at a deeper level.

EMBRACING THE MASCULINE

The masculine energy represents the determination, focus, and drive of Source energy. When balanced with the feminine, it often plays the role of a lover, warrior, or provider. When imbalanced, the lover becomes a liar, the warrior transitions into a worrier, and the provider transforms into a predator. In the absence of a feminine energetic counterpart, the overly masculine ego is more focused on conquering than connecting and far more motivated by the threat of loss than acting upon opportunities to be vulnerable, unguarded, faithful, and intimate.

While the masculine energy can be nurturing as a reliable provider, when imbalanced, an inability to receive fails to fulfill the masculine or allow their partners, friends, and relatives to connect with their heart.

In the most practical sense, the masculine represents goal-oriented focus. It is often described through viewpoints of "what": What am I driven to accomplish? What can I do for you? What can you do for me? What is my purpose?

While focus, drive, and determination are crucial elements in manifesting the soul into tangible form, when imbalanced by the imprinting of our human conditioning or societal pressures, masculine energy can often be aggressive instead of aware. When this occurs, objectivity is replaced with objectification, passion turns to anger, and drive erodes into depression.

As the masculine learns to soften its approach, each goal can be explored for deeper purposes than just conquests, outcomes, or achievements. On a spiritual journey, the masculine is the seeker, pursuer, and interpreter of life's infinite wisdom. Yet it is unable to process, assimilate, and integrate such wisdom without the balance of the feminine energy.

When balanced with its inner feminine counterpart, the masculine learns to provide without needing to protect and to respond instead of react, while becoming a nurturer instead of a neglector. From this space of greater energetic harmony, the masculine is able to surrender into the vulnerability of receiving that allows a person's infinite wellspring of love to be felt by those they adore.

This is why the journey of the masculine involves learning how to equally give and receive with honor, humility, and heartfelt sincerity. When unconscious, this theme serves to awaken the masculine as it learns over time how the negativity it projects outward only creates greater inner conflict. As the masculine awakens to the importance of the Divine feminine, all self-serving tendencies and know-it-all defense mechanisms melt into a greater interest in the well-being of others.

As this occurs, a timeless defender of truth that the masculine so often embodies transforms into a devoted servant of love. How long it takes for such a transition to occur is often determined by how guarded the masculine remains, insisting on protecting the very feminine energy it is unknowingly afraid to let in and fully embrace.

HONORING THE FEMININE

The feminine represents the receptivity, creativity, and nurturing expansion of Source energy. When balanced with the masculine, the feminine often plays the role of an intuitive, parent, and muse. When out of sync with the masculine, the intuitive is overwhelmed in victimhood, and the parent is shrouded in martyrdom, as the muse shuts down in resentment.

In the absence of masculine energy, the feminine is brimming with inspired ideas, while lacking the focus, ambition, and direction to see each inspiration through from concept to creation. While the imbalanced feminine has much love to offer, a reliance on outside validation causes such a nurturing and expanded energy to remain ungrounded, or moving from one chaotic relationship to another.

Even though the feminine radiates the receptivity necessary to create long-lasting intimate relationships, when imbalanced, it is common for the feminine to give all of itself to others at the detriment of its own inner balance. This is why the journey of the feminine energy is learning how to be fearless and faithful in their giving without denying their own needs or losing themselves in the presence of another.

From an energetic standpoint, the feminine balances the goal-oriented male energy, tempering any pursuit or endeavor. While the masculine is geared to define the "what," or objective of a goal, the feminine brings the energy of "how": How will I approach the goal at hand? How often will I follow my own inner guidance? How do I choose to respond to the characters in view? How can I move mindfully toward each goal or pursuit?

While receptivity, creativity, and nurturing expansion are essential components in discovering true wholeness, when imbalanced, feminine energy can often be projected as manipulation instead of mindfulness. When this occurs, depth is replaced with shallowness, forgiveness turns to vengeance, and openness is reduced to apathy.

As the feminine learns to ground its nurturing expansive energy, it softens the masculine. In doing so, it is able to openly receive a depth of intimacy that is equally as honorable to innocence as it is captivating to our senses. Along a spiritual journey, the feminine acts as the intuitive conduit, energetic catalyst, and emotional receiver of Source energy. And yet without the balance of the inner masculine, the feminine expands into higher alignment with the Universe without being able to anchor our energies into tangible physical reality. From this space, the feminine is capable of imagining various solutions but lacks the necessary grounding to act upon such fertile wisdom and engender it into form.

When balanced with the inner masculine, the feminine learns to receive the true joy of intimacy with the utmost self-respect. It is able to foresee intuitions over impulses, while expressing its nurturing expansive power with discerning grace. From this space of energetic balance, the feminine discovers the confidence to unleash its absolute power in the most conscious and heart-centered way.

As this unfolds, the hurtful healer that the suppressed feminine has played out for lifetimes manifests into a sacred expression of alchemy in action. How the feminine transitions from victimhood to victory is determined by how deeply it surrenders to Source and is able to trust the twists and turns of an evolving spiritual journey, no matter how painful a past is to remember or how turbulent the path ahead seems.

ENDING THE WAR OF POLARITY

Whether remembering the Salem witch trials, the Holocaust, executions of artists and authors who spoke out against corrupt political regimes, slavery, the Crusades, or the attacks of 9/11, we can point to countless moments in history when the inner division of polarity has caused the masculine to suppress, dominate, and objectify the power of the Divine feminine. It is important to remember that such persecutions weren't just limited to those of a female gender, but involved all beings who embodied and transmitted the qualities of the inner feminine essence.

More precisely, the history of aggression toward feminine energy can be viewed as acts of persecution against the *innocence* of humanity. The reason why humanity has been the subject of such relentless abuse is due to how the recognition of interconnectedness has been slowly but steadily evolving in human beings since the dawn of time. Because reality was created in an interdimensional hyperspace governed by free will, the evolution of consciousness has expressed and survived some rather brutal precedents as a way of moving the individual and collective awareness toward a more harmonious and heart-centered reality. After generations of corruption, bloodshed, and mistruths projected upon the Divine feminine, we have arrived at a pivotal point in history when the feminine is returning back to equal power in order to temper the masculine.

Whether our energy fields have been encoded with memories of the masculine suppressing the feminine or the feminine rejecting the masculine, we have arrived at an important crossroads. It is where the external conflicts that divide individuals and groups from the sum of the whole can be resolved by bringing the inner masculine and feminine into greater harmonious balance. As each human being balances out their inner polarity of energies, the external play of people, places, and things transforms to reflect a reality of global equality and personal inclusion.

While the main focus of this book is the transition from ego to soul, it also offers keys to balance our masculine and feminine energies, ensuring our shift from WAR to RAW is as balanced as it is expansive. Using the equation of ARE, the first step is always awareness. In becoming more aware of the roles the inner masculine and feminine play, we can take the next step toward greater energetic harmony. To do so, the inner masculine and feminine must come together in resolution, so the fate of our highest expansion may dawn.

Since the masculine energy acts as the determination, focus, and drive of Source energy, it has the ability to make empowered choices that align with higher vibrational realities, once such insights have been received. For this to occur, it is the receptivity, creativity, and nurturing expansion of the inner feminine that becomes the receiver of the knowledge necessary to inspire the masculine into more heart-centered choices.

Using this book as an example, it is the masculine that focuses attention toward the goal of reading every page and exploring each pearl of wisdom. But it is the receptivity of the feminine that absorbs each insight for the masculine to discover.

MELTING EACH BARRIER

In order for the masculine and feminine energies to work together in harmony, we must align with breath on a regular basis to melt any barrier that divides one side from the other. As we learned in Chapter 3, aligning with breath is a way to activate each of the three RAW attributes of respecting, acknowledging, and welcoming—all at once. When we choose to breathe through our experiences, we allow the inner male and female counterparts to enter higher levels of alignment to resolve the patterns of conflict that orbit our fields.

Each inhale represents the receptivity of the feminine, connecting with a sense of strength, courage, and safety. The inhale allows us to cleanse and nourish all levels and layers. The exhale represents the drive of the masculine to respect, acknowledge, and welcome with greater focused intention.

Even if during a busy day we are only able to find pockets of time to take momentary breathing breaks, it is our willingness to turn attention inward toward the power of the breath that dissolves each aspect of incubation for the evolution of the soul. Since the masculine and feminine have both played out roles as victims and victimizers, each cycle of abuse unravels when breathing our way into greater energetic resolution.

Notice how when our conflicts of inner polarity are enacted in the world, the masculine aspect of ourselves cannot suppress, dominate, or objectify the feminine without abandoning the consciousness of our breath.

As the breath is overlooked or subconsciously denied, the imbalanced masculine seeks to project its pain, insecurities, and vulnerabilities onto the innocence of the feminine, attempting to take its breath away.

Equally so, the feminine cannot unconsciously manipulate the masculine as forms of protection or retribution without abandoning its breath as well.

This is why any form of oppression can only occur by turning away from our alignment with breath. Since breathing is the embodied expression of all attributes of RAW, our separation from breath creates the inner WAR of ego, which only the soul's expansion may resolve. Each time we allow our breath to be a central point of focus, we are shifting away from this karmic cycle of abuse—and not just for the reconciliation of our own inner experience but for the expansion of the whole.

Whether we are able to respect, acknowledge, and welcome our way into a more expanded viewpoint or find ourselves worrying, anticipating, and regretting on a recurring basis, we can use the power of the breath to bridge each gap and inspire the soul to emerge.

FROM PERSECUTION TO PARTNERSHIP

Persecution arises when unconscious focus, drive, and determination suppress, dominate, and objectify the innocence of our true nature. This equally can be demonstrated by an imbalanced masculine mind dominating a sensitive feminine heart, just as the conflicts arising between two people. As a way of healing the suppression of the Divine feminine, Source energy takes shape and form as a world of characters within which we clear, activate, and awaken each other's highest potential by way of the forming and dissolving of relationships. While spiritual progress should never be the sole means for developing emotional bonds, the healing that occurs throughout each emotional bond is determined by how much time is spent incubating in ego versus communing as soul.

When two people commune as the soul, unity is discovered. When two people mutually incubate in ego, denial is maintained. When one partner embodies the soul while the other plays out patterns of ego, victimhood is perpetuated.

Whether romantic or fraternal, each relationship serves to heal fractures that once divided the inner masculine from the feminine. As these two polarities come together in harmonious balance, the potential for sacred partnership replaces oscillating patterns of persecution, whether on a physical, mental, emotional, or energetic level.

BECOMING A SACRED PARTNER

As both sides of polarity come together, we are more likely to embody the expansion of our soul in the presence of others. As we become more aligned with Source, and heart-centered in nature, it increases the likelihood that we can attract an external partner who reflects the brightness of the soul back to us.

Creating sacred partnerships—whether with friends, family, acquaintances, or lovers—is a matter of honing the attributes of RAW as gifts that we choose to offer others. Just as the expansion of the soul is determined by unraveling our inner WAR of worry, anticipation, and regret, each external conflict can dissolve when respecting, acknowledging, and welcoming our way throughout each encounter. Moreover, because there is no evolutionary benefit from relationships that perpetuate persecution, it is important, regardless of how others choose to be, that we remain focused on how we respond to others.

RESPECT IN ACTION

As a way to move interpersonal encounters into the possibility of sacred partnership, the attributes of RAW can be externalized, fostering opportunities to commune with the soul while spending time with another.

As the first attribute of RAW, respect is an essential ingredient in raising the vibration of each relationship. Listening is the function of respect in action. When we listen to others, we are verifying the uniqueness of their existence by confirming how worthy they are to be heard as well as seen and received.

While our ego may not always agree with the ideas and opinions suggested, it is important to hear the viewpoint of others, instead of hurrying toward more interesting or agreeable subject matter. We certainly don't have to affirm standpoints that don't resonate with us, but when interacting with others, there is a potential to feel more seen and heard by others, depending upon how actively we see and hear them.

Because reality is governed by the laws of unity consciousness, the attributes of RAW that we offer to others equally expand both souls while resolving any conflicts between the inner masculine and feminine energies. When not consciously respecting, acknowledging, and welcoming as acts of sacred partnership, relationships are more likely to default into interactions of ego, where the inner WAR in both energy fields is maintained.

While the ego tries its best to be an active and engaged listener, listening is a skill set expressed only by the soul. Since the ego can only hear through a self-serving filter, frustrations, inconveniences, and boredom are likely experiences when attempting to listen from a state of incubation.

If you are unable to hear others with sincerity or interest, this indicates a need to make time to hear your inner thoughts, concerns, dreams, and desires more passionately than anyone else's. If this is the case, we are able to expand our capacity to listen to others by first respecting, acknowledging, and welcoming our *own* thoughts and feelings on a deeper level.

Even if that suggestion elicits defensiveness, we can always hone all three attributes of RAW by making time to align with breath. The more often we make time to breathe consciously, the healthier and more fulfilling each partnership can be.

SPEAKING AS SOURCE

As listening creates a foundation for sacred partnership, so the seeds of each bond are given the best opportunity to grow when acknowledgment is offered. As the second attribute of RAW, acknowledgment is an even more engaging next step in listening. It allows those in our lives to be seen and heard, for acknowledgment conveys a sense of value toward a person—whether or not we appreciate the things they say or do.

From the ego's standpoint, no one can be appreciated if we are unable to value the words spoken or the ideologies they represent. From the soul's perspective, each person can be inherently recognized as an expression of Source and offered respect, acknowledgment, and warm welcomes, even when such characters diametrically oppose our highest values and core beliefs.

Acknowledgment is an affirmation or compliment offered to others in response to their sharing. Since our one eternal Source exists as an all-knowing, all-loving, omnipresent force of nature, when responding in complimentary fashion we allow the grace of Source energy to speak through us and touch the lives of others. The more we acknowledge the divinity of others, the more we commune with the light of our own soul.

Even when someone speaks disrespectfully to us, it can become an opportunity to acknowledge and compliment ourselves instead; in doing so, we neutralize the energy of the verbal attack. When we are able to acknowledge the innocence of our own heart or compliment the light of others, no matter how deeply entrenched in a healing journey we are, it is a sign that our ever-expanding soul is stepping forward into the ecstasy of sacred partnership.

Even when we have nothing supportive to say, whenever the gift of listening is offered we can assist in merging the polarity of inner masculine and feminine energies by aligning with breath. Through the Divine attribute of acknowledgment, the more often we focus on the things we and others are doing right, the more we are able to raise the vibration of self-worth in all energy fields.

No matter how deeply entrenched in conflict someone appears to be, the willingness to respond with compliments instead of criticism is a vital way to raise our vibration as announcers of well-being. Noting that whether they choose to receive our acknowledgment may reflect how overwhelmed they are in their own healing journey. Meanwhile, our willingness to open up, even when others lash out or shut down, confirms the beauty of our ever-growing expansion.

AN ALIVENESS OF INTIMACY

As RAW's third attribute, welcoming stabilizes the roots of sacred partnership into fully blossomed potential. Often sensed as an aliveness of intimacy, the soul's ability to welcome remains the instinctive nature in every heart, merely obscured by layers of human conditioning. When aligned with this Divine attribute, each moment can be celebrated as a unique incarnation of experience. Instead of a lifetime being depicted as the birth and death of an individual, each personal encounter contains a specific start and finish, allowing the sum of experiences throughout our day to be a span of many lifetimes. When rooted in welcoming, we are forgiving of the past by allowing each person and circumstance to be welcomed as a brand-new encounter of growth and expansion.

Without effort or fail, the soul is naturally able to allow experiences to be unique, however our past history has been shaped. The ego, however, cannot welcome interactions as brand-new adventures, no matter how hard it tries to get it right. Instead, it holds on to the past by projecting any amount of unprocessed pain onto the characters in view. In daring to meet ourselves and others fresh and new, we discover an inner wellspring of forgiveness that may not forget the past but allows at the same time any character the chance to be better than they have ever been before.

Whether or not they take such an invitation to heart cannot distract from the soul's deepest desire to always respond with more openness for the well-being of all. From this space, we are able to recognize intimacy as the dance through which Source energy meets itself throughout its many faces.

This is where true love is found. It is not merely the electricity of personal arousal but a chance to encounter the light of our divinity as reflected in the beauty of another.

To help you balance out your inner masculine and feminine energies, please consider the wisdom of or repeat aloud the following statement:

I accept that both aspects of polarity are needed in order for the harmony of balance to be. I honor the masculine for its focus, drive, and determination, just as I respect the feminine for its receptivity, creativity, and nurturing expansion. As a way of transforming each relationship into the fulfilling bliss of sacred partnership, I align with my breath to respect, honor, and welcome both sides of my being into greater integrated wholeness.

In balancing my own inner polarity of energies, I assist humanity in breaking cycles of abuse to bring the Divine feminine back into equal power with the masculine. From this space, each moment becomes a fresh opportunity to meet myself and each character fresh and new, without placing myself in toxic environments or unhealthy relationships. And so I am whole.

As the inner masculine and feminine come into greater balance within you, each personal interaction can develop emotional bonds that allow us to enter a space where divinity is naturally recognized. From this space, we are able to honor others as extensions of our true nature, while embracing our *own* hearts as well. This is the awakening of unity consciousness that grows within you through the blossoming of self-love.

CHAPTER 5

THE FOUR FOUNDATIONS OF **SELF-LOVE**

FROM A SPIRITUAL PERSPECTIVE, love isn't an emotion we feel all the time. Love is an unwavering depth of compassion and empathy that reaches inward to embrace our experiences—no matter how mixed up, shut down, unfulfilled, or overwhelmed we tend to be. When rooted in the vibration of love, we don't have to be completely healed in order to bring forth the kindness and care that already dwells within us. Love inspires us to console the innocence within our heart that wishes it felt something other than how things are. Not to be confused with infatuation, true love is a selfless and harmonious response of greater support, not an emotional high of any kind.

The more loving we are in each relationship, the more heart-centered we tend to be. Equally so, the more compassionate we are toward ourselves, the more intimate our relationships can become. This is the recipe for true emotional resolution. In order for each relationship to be aligned with

Source, it is essential to embrace the four foundations of self-love. This embrace transforms each interaction from the inside out, creating more opportunities to meet ourselves in the purity of sacred partnership.

Since we've already explored the first foundation—being more aligned with the breath—we are ready to explore the other three that ensure our highest vibration is cultivated with compassion.

THE GIFT OF SPACE

Love is the magnetic attraction of unity consciousness. While love often arises spontaneously, it can be naturally felt when the gift of space has been received. Whether it is time away from the roles we play, the people we serve, or even from our daily routine, the offering of space occurs anytime we pause for deliberate rest.

While the soul requires moments of spaciousness and rest to remain aligned, the ego is often intimidated by the vulnerability that space reveals.

In the absence of having something to worry about, anticipate, or regret, the gravity of such unconscious tendencies creates a stir of inner restlessness. This discomfort signifies an expansion that illuminates an opening of a previously darkened corner of our inner reality. Space helps us acknowledge our inner patterning, so that a sense of vulnerability can reveal a moment when the ego's only response is to loosen its grip of control.

This is why the ego lives in a divided state of inner conflict. No matter the object of its agenda, it seeks out the very pleasure, validation, and fulfillment that can only be received by the soul. This is because, in order to receive, spaciousness must be present. In the presence of space, the ego unravels.

The ego always wants the very thing it isn't destined or designed to have. Our ego might be able to imagine a particular desire, and it can certainly spend time pursuing it with tremendous force and effort. All the while, each desired outcome is meant to be received as we continue to shift from ego to soul.

Just as food cannot be properly consumed without allowing space for digestion, we cannot be fully aware, aligned, and heart-centered without space. Since space exists as a silent force, the ego desperately tries to avoid it, because it perceives space as loneliness and isolation. On the other hand, the soul honors the gift of space as the environment of solitude where deeper connections are created.

True intimacy is a willingness to be spacious, restful, and open. In sacred partnership, intimacy is an opportunity to share space with another. In order to explore the importance of loving ourselves as an essential component to cultivating sacred partnership, a relationship with space must be established.

This can be as simple as giving ourselves mini mental breaks throughout the day, when we are able to pause, feel our emotional experiences, and even take a few mindful breaths.

Since an alignment with breath invites spaciousness to unravel the ego, it is natural to have a sense of aversion toward space, where nothing but awareness and breath remain. As always, may we take each step of our journey at whatever speed is most supportive. Perhaps it's a matter of finding the edge of our experience and daring to take one step beyond it. Let's say you're waiting in line at the bank, or sitting in traffic. This can be an opportunity to explore spaciousness, instead of worrying, anticipating, or regretting. In big ways and small ways, by stepping toward the gift of space, we are inviting the brightness of the soul to shine through.

MAKING PEACE WITH TIME

The potency of sacred partnership is determined by our relationship with space. When in harmony with spaciousness, we embrace the necessity of resting and receiving, just as we are willing to give and engage. For this to occur, it is essential to make peace with time as the third foundation of self-love. Because the ego is driven to worry, anticipate, and regret, it often lives in a race-against-the-clock scenario. This means everything it wants is always somewhere else or doesn't exist in the way it wishes. The soul, however, naturally exists in a monogamous relationship with space and lives in complete peace with the dimension of time.

As we make peace with time, our inner polarity of energies can balance out more easily. Just as small children can become cranky if they are tired and need a nap, we, too, can quickly escalate into disagreements or misunderstandings when we do not make time for ourselves.

While the ego is bound to unravel as the soul expands, it doesn't let go easily. When making time to cultivate greater inner nourishment, it's like the ego enters emotional rehab. As you go within to become the source of your own loving-kindness, the ego is no longer put in a position to be constantly fed or triggered by the desire for external validation or the approval of others.

In the absence of outside approval, the hunger of ego may intensify, as it fights to remain unconscious through external judgments or patterns of inner criticism. Essentially, when the ego is not fed, it fights back.

All too often, the breakdown of relationships occurs through our unconscious fight with time. We either take others for granted by not spending enough quality time together or we squeeze the intimate space out of our partnerships by not having enough time for ourselves. This is why making peace with time is essential in the cultivation of self-love. When making time to care for ourselves, we are able to make constructive choices, instead of being attracted to self-destructive patterns.

BEING WELL-RESTED

Feeling well-rested is a sign that we have made peace with time. This is the fourth foundation of self-love. As restfulness becomes more regular, we begin to embody the Divine attributes of our highest potential. Without proper rest, we feel displaced, out of sorts, or uneasy about where our lives are headed. Even though there may be evidence to convince us that there is a lot to worry about, such experiences are often signs that more rest is needed.

I have an expression: A couple that is able to *rest together* can be at their *best together.* This is because restfulness helps the roots of relationship grow stronger, allowing the connections between two hearts to align and deepen without personal agenda. Whether we're relating to others or embracing our own inner nature, the foundation of being well-rested is a true measurement of how deeply the gift of space has been received.

When all four foundations are fulfilled—when we're well-rested, rooted in spaciousness, aligned with breath, and at peace with time—we are able to be the most honorable sacred partners to ourselves. And as our inner sacred partnership blossoms, we are able to illuminate the light in others, instead of triggering their ego at every turn.

Since the soul evolves by raising our vibration or through the unraveling of ego, the difference between which roles we play is often reflective in how anchored in self-love we are. If we find ourselves responding with more conflict than compassion on a regular basis, it may be a sign that one of the four foundations is weak or out of balance.

SPACE PLUS TIME EQUALS ATTENTION

Our responses to each of our relationships reflects how rooted we are in heart-centered consciousness. When time and space are allies, instead of enemies, a willingness to give more thoughtful attention becomes a gateway to everlasting fulfillment. This is why the formula for expanding heart-centered consciousness is *space plus time equals attention.*

Without time, attention is limited and conditional. Without space, attention is scattered and unfocused. Therefore, when space and time are aligned in the right relationship through the grace of our renewed clarity and enhanced focus, the things that used to be perceived as barriers become catalysts of expansion.

As we create openings in our lives to provide ourselves the very attention others seem to withhold, a timeless shift from ego to soul naturally occurs. From this space, depending on how aligned we are in the four essential foundations, we are able to be more responsive instead of reactive and more cooperative than competitive.

PASSIVE VERSUS ECSTATIC STATES

A spiritual journey isn't a matter of chasing a bigger transcendent experience but in becoming more sensitive to the subtle energies that always exist within us. As our heart opens, we are able to notice the infinite power that naturally resides in our deepest state of serenity.

From the viewpoint of the ego, bigger experiences are always assumed to be solutions to life's most daunting problems. Often personified as a spiritual adrenaline junkie, the ego attempts to use moments of spiritual expansion as an escape from circumstances it cannot control. Whether through the overuse of plant medicine, dependency on mind-altering drugs, attempting to use healing modalities to feel one way all the time, or even using meditation as a superficial way of checking out of our lives, when mystical experiences occur, whatever degree of ego remains active will develop a hunger for even greater expansion.

Even though the ego will never successfully track down the very outcomes it chases, the pursuit of bigger experiences ensures the ego has something to worry about, anticipate, and regret. It can worry about not ever finding the clarity it yearns to receive, anticipating the arrival of more energetically charged experiences, and even regret the decisions of the past that it imagines are reasons for why its long-awaited spiritual openings have yet to arrive.

From the soul's perspective, ecstatic states of consciousness such as bliss, unity, and love are powerful expressions of the most subtle forces of energy. Bigger spiritual experiences don't necessarily indicate the arrival of a higher vibration. In fact, the most ordinary of circumstances can be witnessed by the highest vibration within us. Since the soul is a manifestation of life's ever-expanding consciousness, it yearns to become as sensitive as possible to the energies taking shape in life. Contrary to the ego that defines itself by the immensity of experiences, the soul focuses on being fully engaged and wholeheartedly receptive to the very moment at hand—no matter how seemingly insignificant.

To the soul, nothing was created without a vital contribution toward our evolution. While the ego may ask each moment, "What can you do for me?" the soul, rooted in sacred humility, asks, "How may I best serve you?"

Even in personal relationships, if the ego is not constantly gratified, showered with fulfillment, and validated at every turn, it feels a sense of rejection from the one who cannot satisfy its insatiable hunger for more. From the viewpoint of the soul, the success of a relationship lies in creating a bond that serves equally the desires of each partner. While the ego often uses partnership to chase after its next big high, the soul is focused on being the most engaging partner, equally giving as well as receiving.

So in order to become more receptive to vivid experiences of Source energy, it is important to understand the relationship between passive and ecstatic states.

THE WAVES AND OCEAN ARE ONE

Passive and ecstatic states maintain a relationship much like how waves are the ongoing activity of an ocean. While waves always churn, they are indivisible parts of one interconnected reality. Just as waves cannot ever be big enough to drown an ocean, no one person or outcome can adversely affect the light of our soul. Instead, it can only limit or contract the ego, as it endures each hardship or sacrifice along its fate of unraveling. If the ocean is a metaphor of Source energy, then each person, place, or thing is a wave of divinity coming and going throughout it.

As we become aligned in the four foundations of self-love, the things in view that once appeared as the highs and lows of everyday life take on a much deeper spiritual meaning. From this oceanic space of heightened receptivity, a willingness to honor the divinity of others becomes a more obvious and natural recognition.

INTEGRATION IS EVERYTHING

The bigger the wave, the more time it takes to dry anything that has been soaked. This is true for spiritual experiences. While the ego believes the greatest relief can only come from the biggest experiences, the soul knows that the more expansive each encounter, the longer it may take to digest, assimilate, and integrate.

We can liken this experience to the recovery process after surgery, when the body may take an extended period of time to adjust to the effects of a medical procedure. Equally so, our energy fields need vital amounts of nurturing, time, and rest to process the transformative effects of each moment of expansion.

A computer is also a good metaphor when observing how our energy field processes the grace of spiritual expansion. Just as a computer requires time to reboot after big files are downloaded, our energy fields go through extensive periods of integration to assimilate all the clearings, activations, and expansions that occur through daily interactions.

If a computer had an ego, it might associate the downloading of big files as sensations of higher spiritual alignment. The moment such downloading is complete, the computer would begin processing each file, which, to its ego, would feel as if the bigger downloading experience had disappeared. If this were so, the ego of a computer would always be downloading, afraid that the moment it stopped, the more expansive state would disappear.

The same is true whenever the ego chases after ecstatic states of consciousness. What the ego often interprets as symptoms that require the resolve of healing modalities are often signs of integration already under way. This means that many of the experiences that cause egos to seek out healing remedies are merely the evidence of integrating greater expansions.

Even if we aren't aware when integration is happening, such Divine subtleties must be assimilated into our energy fields so they can usher us into our next highest stage of evolution.

As a spiritual adrenaline junkie, the ego is addicted and attracted to contrast. When single, the ego dreams of partnership. When in partnership, the ego yearns for the freedom of being single. No matter the example, the ego tends to believe that changes in environment are the only way to feel better. Even though it is the integration of the soul that unravels the ego, the ego is able to notice the initial flow of expanding energy. Once the rush of emotional contrast fades, a process of integration begins.

Instead of feeling energized and uplifted as we may have during the arrival of greater expansion, during integration we may feel tired, depleted, melancholy, or desire to withdraw.

While the ego believes spiritual experiences shift everything in a split second, it doesn't have the capacity to respect the equally important process of integration. This is because the very integration under way is the force through which the ego returns to Source. If the ego seeks healing, it is only to maintain the patterns of conditioning that integration resolves.

It is why the four foundations of self-love are so instrumental to our spiritual journey. Instead of perceiving barriers throughout life, we are able—well-rested, rooted in spaciousness, aligned with breath, and at peace with time—to recognize opportunities to assist the proper assimilation of Source energy.

As we become a more engaged participant in the expansions and integrations already in progress, we are likely to be more receptive to a deeper spiritual reality—instead of chasing after bigger experiences that only ensure longer periods of rest. While eating delicious food can provide a moment of instant gratification, the body goes through a much longer process in order to digest it. In the same way, a momentary expansion of awareness may feed the ego with the contrast it desires, but it also calls into action a much longer period of rejuvenation and renewal.

This is why there is no need to chase after the spiritual experiences that our ego may crave. In allowing everything to come to us, precisely at the moment it's meant to be, we are ensured to have perfectly aligned openings in consciousness that integrate with harmony and ease. For this to happen, we must become respectful and welcoming to the world of subtle energy. We know from the depths of our soul it is the most gentle experiences that, when embraced from the highest vibration of consciousness, reveal the deepest wisdom and the bigger, most memorable, cosmic picture of our destiny.

THE EGO NEEDS LOVE

One of the reasons why being aligned in the four foundations assists in the integration of ego is that in order for it to unravel, it must be loved. While the ego may remember rejections of the past, it cannot be integrated if rejected in any way.

Equally so, giving in to each and every desire cannot provide the ego with the emotional nourishment that assists in completing its journey. As easy as it is to dislike how life feels during incubation—the time we spend in ego before the soul begins to awaken and expand—it is essential to be firmly rooted in the four foundations. We need to develop compassion and empathy for the ego, whether arising within ourselves or playing out in others. Otherwise, we may develop a more slippery and elusive spiritual ego. When this occurs, we tend to find fault and conflict with other egos. We may try using healing modalities to attain bigger energetic experiences to hide from a reality we came to transform.

This shows how emotional receptivity is a timeless gateway into transcendent spiritual realities. While the ego seeks transcendence to turn away from difficult feelings, it is the reconciliation of our emotions that grants us access to life's deepest revelations. As our vibration elevates, a capacity to embody and transmit well-being amplifies. This means the more emotionally receptive we become, the higher the frequencies of light we can welcome into awareness and bring forth for others.

While the ego judges each feeling solely on how painful or pleasant it is, the soul views each emotion while it lasts as an opportunity to love itself. No matter how frustrating, inconvenient, or boring an experience may seem, instead of trying to change how it feels we are changing the way we view and respond.

As lightbearers of a new reality, we dare to give the innocence of our emotions more thoughtful attention as acts of self-love. Even when we don't wish to embrace the ego, it can become a fertile opportunity to be more restful, rooted in spaciousness, aligned with breath, and at peace with time than ever before.

To help embody the four foundations of self-love, please consider the wisdom of or repeat aloud the following statement:

I accept that resolution is not determined by bigger spiritual experiences but by allowing the subtlest of energies to be embraced by the highest vibration of consciousness already within me. This occurs by embracing the four foundations of self-love as a way of helping me integrate the healing journey already under way.

As I take the time to be well-rested, rooted in spaciousness, aligned with breath, and at peace with time, I deepen my own sacred partnership with myself. From this space, emotional receptivity becomes a gateway into transcendent spiritual experiences that come to me much faster than I can chase after them. As this occurs, I am elevating my vibration as an announcer of well-being to inspire the world to be more caring and compassionate, just by taking time to nurture myself. And so I am embraced.

When the integration process can be as equally respected as our desires for expanded states or mystical experiences, the wisdom and maturity of an awakening soul has dawned. From this space, we are able to notice the difference between what we want and the things we need with a willingness to embrace the climate of our current realities as the unfolding of our most triumphant transformation.

CHAPTER 6

THE
GOLDEN
QUESTION

ON AN EMOTIONAL LEVEL, a shift from ego to soul is transforming the aggression of overreactivity into the diplomacy of conscious response. This occurs through the five stages of surrender that we will soon discuss in this book.

To set the stage for deep, heartfelt surrender in Chapter 7, one of the most profound spiritual insights is meant to be embraced so deeply that it changes the way we interact with reality. It is much like crossing a point of no return, where the one taking the leap isn't the one landing on the other side. Metaphorically speaking, a transformation occurs in midair, exchanging the ego that attempts to cross such a threshold for the soul that only exists in the aftermath. While the metaphor of a leap might seem like a quick shift, each of us is encoded with the privilege of a journey that unfolds as suddenly or as slowly as we need it to be.

The ego is either motivated to speed toward a destination or control the fate of outcomes. However, each experience is in fact a gift to be unwrapped, savored, and enjoyed from start to finish. The ego can only enjoy moments that match its preferences; the soul is able to access a much deeper reality.

To begin our journey of surrender, it is essential to embrace every living thing as an expression of Source energy. Whether this seems like an overstated spiritual insight or a concept we may not have directly experienced, the depth to which this truth is honored determines the course of our mastery.

THE ESSENCE OF FORGIVENESS

In the heart of surrender, what we perceive as personal criticism from others is our own judgment of someone else's pain. While it is easy to interpret someone's judgment of you as an attack, at a deeper glance we see someone so entrenched in a healing journey they may not understand that their only recourse for momentary relief is to project their frustrations onto others. When aligned with Source energy, we don't have to be victims of other people's abuse in order to hold space for their healing. Equally so, we can welcome interactions with even our harshest critics, who perhaps have only been delivered into our reality to help soften a few more edges.

Perhaps the soul is like a slab of marble. The people seeming to attack with verbal or emotional weapons are the tools of a Divine artist, used to shape us into the works of art we're destined to be. This reveals true forgiveness as a chance to pardon each character for the actions at hand, while our highest potential is molded, polished, and shined to completion.

To access the essence of forgiveness, please consider the insights of the following questions:

What if things can happen without blaming any particular character?

What if there can be pain, hurt, heartbreak, and betrayal without associating it with the characters playing out each action?

What if blaming characters is a way of separating from Source?

What if returning to Source occurs by pardoning the characters attached to my most painful memories?

What if Source orchestrated each and every scenario beyond the notion of reward and punishment?

What if I tend to believe in reward and punishment because I was once blamed by others for the actions of Source?

What if Source only created each scenario to inspire a journey of redemption to uplift and heal the world around me?

What occurs when each and every opinion, judgment, or conclusion is returned to Source?

WE WERE NEVER THE TARGET

While each of us has survived the unsuspecting plight of human suffering in one form or another, there exists a much deeper reason why things happen the way they do. As expressions of Source energy, we incarnated onto a planet where each outcome and interaction offers practical opportunities to apply all the wisdom of heaven.

Since forgiveness begins by remembering each perpetrator as a messenger of divinity, the essence of forgiveness deepens as we also acknowledge *ourselves* as Source energy dressed up as characters in view. When remembering our true nature, we begin to unhook from our identification as victims, simply because we were never the target of anyone's attack. Our experiences of pain, despair, and confusion were really the varying degrees of separation that *humanity* has experienced.

In truth, we are the light of divinity. We are experiencing the unconsciousness of the world that we came to transform as a stage within the healing journey that unfolds through our survival of each hardship. Before we are able to heal the planet, we must first get to know the patterns at play. This occurs by being placed in microcosms of the collective ego structure otherwise known as families. Throughout our up-bringing, we underwent a conditioning process to become just like the characters around us so that we might learn the patterns that Source incarnated to resolve.

To the ego, this can seem cruel or unfair—and might even create resentment toward the Universe. But life should be viewed as a multidimensional movie. Instead of passing judgment on the outcomes of the first few scenes, our soul settles in for a journey of a lifetime. In doing so, it allows the second and third act of life's epic saga to be a redemptive payoff for the circumstances created at the beginning of the storyline.

Every attack is the ego's unconscious denial of its own divinity in form. Each abuse is the ego's attempt to control and dominate. Any rejection is the ego turning away from Source whenever it doesn't get its way.

Although we may have begun our journey as a victim of circumstances, each pain and hardship serves our highest expansion as we remember the light of divinity masquerading in every form. Such healing deepens as we recognize how Source energy only endures the nature of hardship to set up a more profound healing journey for the well-being of all. Even though we will be the first character to expand, over an auspicious period of time each person, place, and thing begins to soften in view, as the world reflects back the higher vibration of consciousness we cultivate.

While we cannot be personally blamed for the unconsciousness of humanity, we have incarnated onto Earth to participate in a collective transformation of reality. As this unfolds, the truth of Source energy awakens, not just in select individuals but on a global level. This may help us acknowledge the power of our personal journey as one of our greatest contributions toward the healing of this planet.

Perhaps the essence of forgiveness is remembering life as an interactive movie of Source meeting Source only for the purposes of expanding the storyline and transforming each character. As forgiveness ripens our heart for the deepest surrender to occur, anything we have done to others or others have done to us can be healed instead of harbored.

To allow the essence of forgiveness to help prepare us for the five levels of surrender, please consider the insights of the following questions:

What would my life be like if I held nothing against myself or others?

What if the least redeeming qualities and actions of any character reflect how deeply entrenched in ego they happen to be?

Is it possible that unconscious behavior or the cruelty of others had nothing to do with me?

Can I see each moment of despair as evidence of humanity's separation from Source?

Am I ready to heal myself as one of the greatest contributions toward the evolution of Earth?

What if my deepest surrender is occurring to help make it easier for others to awaken?

What if life were far too perfect to be unfair?

Am I willing to move forward in the storyline of reality and see how everything comes together for my highest evolutionary benefit?

Can I forgive myself and others as a way of aligning with the perfection of Source?

As the grip of victimhood loosens, we see our world through brand-new eyes. This means we are able to see deeper opportunities in each moment than how scenes may be scripted. When daring to live for the evolution of the world, it's amazing how less scary a place it seems to be. When we're not incubating in ego, we don't shut down and remain stuck in the past.

Since we have already survived the insurmountable odds that life has brought our way, now is the time to put all the pieces together to discover the wholeness that liberates all.

THE SOUL ALWAYS EVOLVES

One of the most intriguing qualities of the soul is its resilience and determination to evolve under any circumstances. The ego believes inner growth only occurs on its precise terms and conditions. It's as if the ego is only willing to evolve when it feels like it! While we don't always have to be uncomfortable in order to expand, we also don't have to hold ourselves back from a reality that only invites us to shine.

It is our innermost desire to allow each outcome to shape us into the works of art that we are destined to be and that confirm our highest angelic vibration in consciousness.

In order to do so, it is essential to shift out of the very ego structure that life is bound to deconstruct. The less life has to unravel, the more pleasantly and harmoniously our journey can unfold. While many people attempt to unravel their egos as quickly as possible, such an outcome-based agenda usually only creates *more* patterns to resolve. To liberate the ego, the wisest and most loving approach is always the best one.

The four foundations of self-love, which we explored in Chapter 5, can now create the fertile ground for our deepest heartfelt surrender. It is not a matter of abandoning the ego. It is more a willingness to release it, much like a butterfly metamorphosing from a caterpillar and being set free from its cocoon. When shifting from ego to soul, a journey of surrender means daring to open up and step forward into the mystery of life, and instead of imagining one fateful moment of resignation, it can be depicted progressively through five distinct stages.

EXPLORING THE GOLDEN QUESTION

One of the five stages of surrender is the Golden Question. As always, when contemplating such an energetically encoded inquiry, it isn't a matter of searching for an "answer." It's more centered in *feeling*. With openness, silence, serenity, and expansion, we can listen, consider, and reflect on the wisdom of the Golden Question.

The Golden Question can be asked as a daily spiritual practice or applied during moments of stress. No matter how it is called to be applied, it assists us in unhooking from the burden of victimhood by considering a viewpoint that only the soul can see. The Golden Question invites us to consider:

What if the worst things that ever happened to me were the greatest opportunities I have ever been given?

In order to fully grasp such wisdom, we remember the soul's primary focus. From the soul's point of view, it is more important to reflect and respond openly than to feel victimized. In essence, with our ego, we tend to default into viewpoints of victimhood or WAR when we are not aware of the benefits and opportunities each moment provides.

Whether finding time to respect, acknowledge, and welcome each circumstance on a deeper level—or by making more empowered choices that further our alignment within the four foundations—each moment can become a profound step forward, depending on how we choose to respond.

FINDING TRUE SAFETY

As a result of the experiences we've had, it is quite natural to feel unsafe in the world around us. However, from the soul's perspective, just by enduring each harsh outcome—whether it seems cruel, senseless, or completely justified—we gain the gifts of evolutionary benefit. Each gift rests dormant in our energy fields, like a hidden savings account that accrues wealth. This wealth is a deeper enlightenment. Contrary to the old spiritual paradigm that believes evolution only occurs to those who are always on their best emotional behavior, the new paradigm offers a more inclusive view.

Whether we responded consciously or not to these unforeseen, unavoidable circumstances, just by *having* these experiences the transformative benefits are already encoded within us. However, the cultivation of heart-centered consciousness allows these gifts from our past and future to be recognized and integrated more fully into our daily lives.

Once all of our dormant gifts have been awakened and received, there exists no past to resolve.

This is why the soul recognizes safety as a sense of inner freedom; it stems from taking pride in the unthinkable moments we had the power to survive. Unlike the soul, the ego perceives safety as a long-lost jewel grasped from its grip by unjust outcomes.

Of course, no matter which perspective seems true right now, we certainly don't have to like what torments we may have endured. Equally, we can always acknowledge the infinite power of Source energy that miraculously guided us beyond our darkest hour.

If we have the awareness to contemplate the expansion of the soul, we are far safer than we may think. Those who still exist in unsafe environments or toxic relationships may not have the time or capacity to consider their spiritual evolution. But the fact that you are here, reading these words, confirms a depth of safety, and a willingness to unveil our highest victory.

While the ego believes it cannot evolve until it feels safe, the soul knows that finding true safety is not physical, but spiritual. It is the end result of our willingness to evolve. Simply by asking the Golden Question—*What if the worst things that ever happened to me were the greatest opportunities I have ever been given?*—an inner awakening occurs.

Since the ego cannot exist outside of the inner WAR of incubation, it can only use such a question to create more regret. The ego can recognize moments of pain and misfortune—and even intellectually know that heartbreak can contain greater purposes—but because those moments exist in the past, the ego stays isolated in guilt and shame, imagining such growth to be lost opportunities.

While the worst moments may be far behind us, the evolutionary benefits gathered from the past are ready to be activated the moment our heart opens. The more often we align in the four foundations of self-love, the easier it is to recognize the most powerful and always available choices.

The sooner our lives become a canvas for the artistry of our most courageous decisions, the more beautiful each moment can be. In the presence of Divine beauty, our heart-centered alignment with Source energy provides us with the safety, support, and encouragement that no person, place, or thing can ever guarantee. While the ego dwells on the past as outcomes that should never have occurred, the soul faces forward with no need to look back.

Instead, now that the past has come and gone, the soul requests the guidance and grace of Source to mold it into its highest form.

FEELING OUR FEELINGS

Whether integrating expansions in consciousness that appear as a healing crisis or yearning to break free from the incubation of ego, the evolution of the soul occurs at the rate at which we become more heart-centered in nature. To be more rooted in our hearts is the courage of emotional receptivity. In order to be more receptive and responsive, instead of critical and reactive, the new paradigm highlights the importance of feeling our feelings. As we make peace with our emotions, we discover an unwavering sense of safety, within which we may be freely alive and at full capacity in the world.

All too often the ego attempts to face emotions through various imbalances in masculine and feminine energies. When imbalanced in the masculine, the ego overthinks each sensation, assuming that having a greater understanding of each feeling can extinguish the discomfort. When imbalanced in the feminine, the ego is overwhelmed by feelings, often lashing out or shutting down in response to emotional triggers. When the inner polarities of energy are balanced, the soul steps forward to experience each sensation in a way that honors and respects the emotional debris purged out of our energy fields.

Negative feelings offer us an opportunity to clear out layers of conditioning that we have carried for lifetimes. Meanwhile, the arising of positive emotions confirms the activation of dormant gifts provided from the past. As we make peace with each feeling, allowing emotional triggers to inspire a greater cultivation of RAW, we are able to clear the necessary space for greater expansion out of our energy fields.

This doesn't mean we will never have an outburst or be triggered by others. Instead, we may find our emotions to be more consistently balanced, while possessing the awareness to feel without overthinking, lashing out, or shutting down.

Because the path of surrender is the very process through which we shift from ego to soul, it is natural for emotional surges to erupt. As we learn to experience this shift from the soul's perspective, each memory that surfaces becomes a vital opportunity to further establish sacred partnership with our own innocence of heart. Perhaps this means being the type of parent we may have always wanted, becoming the friend who is always there for us—even speaking to our heart as our own eternal beloved.

As we dare to open up, even under the most dire emotional circumstances, we invite the perfection of Source energy to transform us for the well-being of all.

TRUE EMOTIONAL FREEDOM

Facing our feelings is a matter of experiencing sensations from the soul's perspective. From this viewpoint, the soul separates each emotional response from the characters that appear to trigger them. Inherently, this is forgiveness in action. Once we are able to be attentive to each feeling without blame, each sensation is given the unwavering attention of unconditional love, facilitating deeper levels of healing.

Nearly opposite to the soul's perspective, the ego cannot feel without judgment or blame. As a collection of unconscious conditioning, the ego is unable to separate effect from cause, which maintains the nature of personal suffering by identifying with our healing journey instead of transforming it.

While the ego is to be respected as the soul in its most dormant phases of expansion, it works tirelessly to *impersonate* the qualities of the soul that so effortlessly rise to the surface as we awaken heart-centered consciousness.

To either begin or further your awakening, simply repeat the following words, either silently or aloud. As always, it is essential to tune in to the visceral feelings of the body's infinite wisdom to confirm our highest knowing.

I accept that my role in the expansion of my energy field, the healing of my body, and the awakening of my consciousness occurs by separating my feelings from the characters I believe cause me to feel this way. Instead of believing any person has made me feel however I feel, I accept that any character can only bring to light the clusters of emotions that have always dwelled within me, simply waiting for the perfect moment in time to be resolved. By acknowledging any belief of judgment or blame as a by-product of unconscious conditioning, I hereby break the cycle of abuse, victimhood, and codependency from all aspects of my energy field and reality. While I may feel as if others are to blame, I recognize it as patterns of ego that cry out for my loving attention as they unravel and integrate into the light of my Divine heart space. I further acknowledge that emotional debris has only been dormant in my energy field, as my contribution to raising the vibration of humanity by healing the emotions I gathered from my family.

In knowing it is so, I allow all energies, beliefs, imprints, genetic lineages, ancestral patterning, unconscious conditioning, and cellular memories that are not mine and do not belong to me, which I was born to resolve, to be cleared out of this energy field, returned to the Source of their origin, and transmuted completely for the well-being of all. From this moment forward, I surrender to the light of my highest Divine authority, able to welcome any emotion as an opportunity to allow my love to become more unconditional than ever before.

I no longer require suffering in order to grow, now that I no longer associate my feelings with characters in view. From this moment forward, I no longer enable others to ignore their own light by disrespecting me. I accept the awareness already awake within me that knows when to move on from relationships and open up space for higher vibrational realities based on the conduct of those in view.

With this declaration, I hereby reclaim my complete and absolute power, stand tall in recognizing and acting upon my highest truth, and step forward as a living anchor of heart-centered consciousness. And so it is.

No matter how convincing our perceptions or feelings may be, when we no longer associate truth as the linking of feelings with characters or events, we are able to heal emotional wounds on a cellular level, while assisting humanity in seeing through the veil of separation.

Even if the actions of characters don't feel good to us, it is either an opportunity to surrender the tendency of blame, or a sign that such relationships have lived out their highest purpose and no longer serve us in our journey ahead. The answer is determined by the clarity of our consciousness. This can be measured by how many people we tend to blame. The fewer people we blame, the clearer our consciousness becomes. Even if there is just one person we continue to blame, our evolution pauses until such a belief is surrendered. This is the heart of true emotional freedom.

To help embody the insights of the Golden Question, please consider the wisdom of or repeat aloud the following statement:

I accept that everything is here to help me, no matter how inconvenient, painful, confusing, or frustrating it seems to be. Through the wisdom of the Golden Question, I allow the worst things that have ever happened to me to be embraced as the greatest opportunities I've been given to grow and evolve.

By separating the effect of my feelings from blaming the characters who seemed to cause them, I allow my emotions to be felt wholeheartedly, as a contribution toward my own healing journey, as well as the expansion of all. From this space of greater safety, I activate the power of true forgiveness by pardoning the characters in view and reminding myself that I wasn't the actual target of any attack.

Instead, I am witnessing the many ways in which Source energy returns to its true nature throughout the awakening of every heart. This completes my first stage in the journey of surrender, which ushers me into an exciting new chapter of my journey, where there is everything to embrace and nothing to blame. And so I am redeemed.

To recap our journey so far, the new paradigm of spiritual evolution is an exploration into heart-centered consciousness. It is a timeless shift from ego to soul that occurs when awareness combines with resolution to inspire greater energetic expansion. First, we become aware of the three activities of ego, followed by the resolution to cultivate light by honing the RAW qualities of the soul. As the patterns of inner WAR are transformed by the actions of RAW, each perceivable enemy can become a spiritual ally in disguise.

When this occurs, allies represent milestones of spiritual evolution, as well as patterns of emotional debris that we are clearing out of ourselves and those around us. As we learn to respect, acknowledge, and welcome simultaneously through the power of the breath, we balance out our inner masculine and feminine energies to transform personal conflict into the beauty of sacred partnership.

To help further the blossoming of sacred partnership within and throughout, we continue to expand the brightness of our soul by aligning with the four foundations of self-love. When ready to be as integrated as we are expanded, the victimhood of ego is deconstructed through the five stages of surrender. Beginning with the Golden Question, we dare to consider how the worst moments of our lives have been some of the greatest opportunities to expand and grow. As we dare to evolve in the most heart-centered way, we are not just transforming our individual realities, but also contributing toward the collective tipping point that awakens the world as ONE.

CHAPTER 7

THE FIVE
STAGES OF
SURRENDER

WHILE THE EGO REMAINS tortured by the necessity of surrendering control to the silent and often unexplainable hands of fate, the ups and downs of your journey exist as the soul's most exciting and rewarding course of mastery. The reason why the ego cannot ever successfully surrender is because it is the very thing *being surrendered*. While the ego works toward surrendering, often viewing the Universe through a lens of reward and punishment, the closest it can get is admitting, "I don't know how."

When "I don't know" can be embraced, it signifies a readiness for the deeper path of spiritual evolution. It's much like the energy of a relay runner who senses the baton they carry is meant to be handed over to the next runner as they complete their leg of the race. It's a giving up, and a letting go. Admitting what we don't know is the ultimate release. When this is experienced from the ego's point of view, it can often feel like guilt, shame, depression, or a sense of worthlessness.

While the ego views the unknown as a great loss or void, the soul experiences each moment of unsuspecting change as the end of the old and the *beginning* of something new.

When we are aligned with the soul, we don't have to be excited about the prospects of devastation, loss, or not knowing in order to remain open to the fate of infinite potential. From the soul's point of view, people, places, and things are costumes that Source wears, only playing the exact role to help our light come out of hiding. When lost in ego, life is a stressful pursuit of seeking pleasure to avoid the burden of pain. As this occurs, each character is judged by the actions that have been orchestrated on a level of reality beyond the notion of individual choice.

Whether in the aftermath of loss or at the brink of personal despair, a readiness to surrender occurs through moments of "I don't know." It doesn't mean we walk around refusing to understand, shirking our responsibilities, or pushing away the pearls of insight that come to us. It is more an ease of serenity in which we can be honest about our pain while remaining open to a process that goes far beyond beliefs of fairness or right and wrong.

To prepare for the five stages of surrender, please consider the wisdom of the following questions as a way of embracing the beauty of "I don't know." As always, merely read each question, whether silently or aloud, and feel into the truth of a more expanded viewpoint.

Why do I need to know what I don't right now?

What if having a deeper knowing won't change how I feel?

What if everything comes to mind at the exact moment it is meant to be known?

Am I willing to trust more of what I don't know than the things I insist to be true?

What would this moment be like if I allowed myself to be open with nothing more in need of being known, resolved, or clarified?

Can I see how even when I'm given a deeper knowing, it only creates a hunger to know more?

When has knowing ever led me to not needing to know?

Will I allow life to know everything on my behalf and bring me each insight on its precise terms and conditions?

Whether you feel an openness and relaxation in response to each question or you get triggered emotionally, embracing the beauty of "I don't know" offers an initial step out of the prison cell of personal belief.

STAGE 1: THE END OF PERSONAL ABANDONMENT

While some of our deepest wounds come from feeling abandoned by others, it is surprising to see how often we abandon *ourselves* through the way we view life. It's natural to perceive through a lens of blame at the moment of emotional impact, but each stage of surrender offers us time and space to regroup and open our viewpoints for our highest evolutionary benefit.

It's okay to feel wronged by people or traumatized by circumstances. This reveals anger as a faithful guardian reminding us how overwhelmed we are by the outcomes at hand. While we will inevitably use each trauma as a catalyst for our deepest growth, such anger informs us when the highest importance is being attentive to our own experiences like a faithful companion.

As waves of emotion begin to settle, we may ask ourselves, "Although I feel wronged, what am I going to do about it?" Will we allow experiences of disappointment or even cruelty to inspire our most courageous decisions and willingness to evolve?

When viewing others as characters who have wronged us, a moment of personal abandonment occurs. Instead of remaining present to the sheer devastation we feel, a need to align with ego can occur through the blaming of others.

While it seems nearly instinctive to see life as the comings and goings of how people treat us, when focused on cultivating our most Divine qualities, pain often confirms how quickly we are shifting from ego to soul. From the soul's perspective, pain represents the initial steps out of the identity and reference points of an old reality as we make our way into a brand new paradigm of being. The more this process is attempted to be rushed, the more insufferable it becomes.

> **To end the agony of personal abandonment, we enter the first stage of surrender by asking the following question:**
>
> *Am I seeing this moment in a way that helps or hurts me?*

From the standpoint of ego, life is a play of me versus you or us versus them. But from the soul's perspective, characters are like instruments that help develop and uncover the melody of our highest vibration. Even when the friction of conflict seems to divide people, as souls we are working together to play out the exact roles to clear, activate, and awaken our true radiance. The more aligned in Source energy we become, the easier each moment of transformation tends to feel. This doesn't mean we are immune to disappointment, heartbreak, or devastation. Instead, we are keenly aware of how often life is giving us the chance to grow and expand. A willingness to be stretched and re-created into a more refined form is a testament to the fiercely liberated nature of our soul.

To the ego, the soul's willingness to grow under the threat of any circumstance seems foolish, shortsighted, and insane. This is because the ego can only interpret that reality as worry, anticipation, and regret.

During such stages of incubation, there is little to no awareness of taking responsibility for our view of things. This is because we are often too overwhelmed by the pain of loss and the anxious despair of unavoidable change.

Throughout the first stage of surrender, we respect the gravity of our feelings, acknowledge each thought, belief, or conclusion as having a right to exist, and welcome each experience—no matter how surreal, one-sided, or distasteful it seems. This occurs by relinquishing any tendency of personal abandonment by focusing on whether we are helping or hurting our experience by the way we view it.

While people, places, and things come and go in their own rhythm and trajectory, they are woven in and out of our reality as instigators of change. The more willing we are to show ourselves unwavering emotional support, the less likely we are to make the actions of others the reason for our pain.

STAGE 2: DISSOLVING ATTACHMENT

Surrender is a willingness to become unstuck. All too often, the barrier to such clarity, peace, and freedom is an *attachment* to things looking or acting in a specific way. While it is wonderful when the inevitabilities of life match our deepest desires, we are not meeting each moment in freedom when we need it to exist solely on our personal terms and conditions.

When we are attached to an outcome, understanding becomes argumentative, communication creates conflict, and benevolence turns to blame. As attachments dissolve, we are able to wholeheartedly embrace the depths of our own experience, while honoring the truth of others, no matter how drastically it differs from ours.

In ego, we insist on being right in the minds of others. As the soul, we allow everyone to be heard without needing anyone to change their position or viewpoint.

In order to advance to the next stage of surrender, it is important to unravel the three prime attachments that bind us in ego. They are explored by considering the following question:

What am I afraid to admit, lose, or gain?

Asking such a question is a way of seeing through the facade of symbolism. It is the difference between the way things are and what they personally mean to you. While an apple pie from the store can have a similar aroma to one your grandmother made, if you take a bite of it, that doesn't mean you are actually eating a slice of her pie. As we wake up from the dream of symbols, everything is given the freedom to exist without becoming a representation of personal meaning that perhaps we alone have created.

Relationships are always a perfect example. While a marriage symbolizes the commitment between two partners, it can only be an establishment of connection for as long as both people are willing. When one no longer feels the way the other one does, it can signify the transformation or even the dissolving of a relationship, depending on how it's symbolized. If a partner defines our existence, what happens to our existence if that partnership ends?

In ego, realities crumble as symbols change. It can be disillusioning to discover that what something has always symbolized for us may mean something entirely different to someone else. It often leads to moments of profound exasperation, where the person you knew and loved has now changed, for better or worse. Instead of honoring the pain of loss or supporting their changing of ways, we tend to grasp onto each symbol to keep it intact as a way of avoiding the devastation of an unraveling ego.

As a way of dissolving our attachments to symbols—so we can meet reality as it is—we set aside the tendency to tell ourselves what things mean: We can dare to experience each moment without drawing conclusions. What if the ending of a career didn't have to symbolize a threat against our livelihood? What if the dissolving of a relationship didn't mean the death of love? What if betrayal didn't indicate anything less than about us? What if another person's opinion had nothing to do with how we view ourselves or them?

In the heart of surrender, we come to see that we tend to oppose outcomes or deny circumstances because of how they change, limit, or distort our sense of self. When rooted in ego, our inner value comes and goes like emotional weather patterns of ever-changing circumstance. From the soul's point of view, we are not angry, hurt, or disappointed due to each outcome, but because of what we believe is true about us, as a result of each occurrence.

This is why the second stage of surrender asks, *What am I afraid to admit, lose, or gain?*

To explore the second stage of surrender at an even deeper level, please consider the wisdom of the following questions:

What am I afraid to admit will be true about myself when and if things don't go my way?

What am I afraid is true about me that makes me feel ashamed and causes me to overcompensate in life just to prove that belief wrong?

What's the most painful thing I believe about myself when no one is looking?

What defines my sense of self that I am the most afraid to lose?

Who do I think I'd be without it?

Whether a disease, enemy, debt, or any type of adversity, what's the worst thing I am afraid to face?

What conclusions would I draw if I were to encounter it?

How does life change when I see each thing as an individual creation, instead of what it personally symbolizes or means to me?

As each person, place, and thing becomes a living expression of Source energy, instead of a reflection of our most limiting ideas, we are able to meet the truth of reality, whether appearing to serve our needs or conspiring against us. From this space, we no longer use the actions of others to inspire self-criticism, while allowing gains and losses to come and go without a desperate grip.

STAGE 3: MOVING BEYOND LIMITING BELIEFS

As part of the five stages of surrender, the Golden Question asks: *What if the worst things that ever happened to me were the greatest opportunities I have ever been given?*

Such a huge shift in perspective allows enough space for our experiences to breathe, instead of being stifled by the symbols projected upon them. Each time it's considered, the Golden Question helps us face life without a need to confine it as an image, or wedge it into a frame of thought.

As we become more aligned with Source, what may have been true before doesn't have to be true now, since reality takes shape and form on a path of ever-growing expansion.

Whether you and another person are meant to grow together or inevitably drift apart, it is a timeless journey that has already been written across all galaxies. Whichever version or timeline we encounter is solely dependent upon how much ego has dissolved and how profoundly our soul can expand. This is precisely why other people are spiritual allies along the soul's journey. Whether depicted in mind as friends, foes, victims, or victimizers, they have been delivered into our reality to inspire profound shifts.

In order to reap the most rewards from each encounter without denying the importance of our deepest feelings, we dare to see through the imprinting of our most limiting beliefs.

> **To explore reality outside of the distorted view of limiting beliefs, please consider the wisdom of the following questions:**
>
> *What have the actions of others caused me to falsely believe about myself?*
>
> *What was the most hurtful thing anyone ever said or did that caused me to feel unworthy, unwelcomed, or unsafe?*
>
> *What has my past led me to conclude?*
>
> *What person, place, or thing triggers the most limiting response in me?*
>
> *Why do the actions of other people have the power to determine my experiences?*
>
> *What would my life be like beyond the notion of right or wrong?*
>
> *Am I afraid that without the false protection of limiting beliefs, I'll be a bigger target for pain, rejection, and misfortune?*
>
> *What evidence or ideas do I use to justify hiding, shutting down, pulling back, or turning away?*

As such questions are considered, it is natural to feel the inner grip of attachment beginning to dissolve. It is where the inner landscape of our energy field opens up space for the RAW qualities of the soul to emerge.

STAGE 4: THE GRACE OF DEVASTATION

In order to fully align with the wisdom and grace of Source, it is important to trust its guidance on an unconditional level. Whether it's following a gut instinct or just being willing to open ourselves up to change, the more we trust the light of our own divinity, the easier it is for the soul to expand. Even when the circumstances of reality seem to be imploding with magnificent precision, trust offers opportunities to explore our deepest surrender through greater leaps of faith.

Instead of trusting Source, despite how elusive, invisible, or intangible it seems to be, we often align with the most limiting beliefs, ideas, and choices that maintain the torment of emotional pain. When the fate of our expansion needs to break open greater space and perspective, it spares no expense in dismantling each blockage of imprinting that we so often perceive as ourselves.

In order to allow the grace of our most devastating hardships to bring us into communion with Source energy, instead of confirming our most limiting beliefs, the fourth stage of surrender can be explored through the following question:

Am I willing to be devastated in order to reveal the deepest truth within me?

While it's natural to desire something new, it's a far grittier undertaking to allow the old to be dismantled as a way of creating fresh space. We may not need to be devastated at every turn, but as long as we are willing to be completely blindsided, uprooted, disappointed, and in some cases even betrayed, we are offering absolute faith to our deepest truth.

Such devastation may require unsuspecting change or the unsavory actions of others, seemingly without any degree of remorse. Whether in response to a job loss, divorce, the diagnosis of an illness, or even the loss of a loved one, this is not done to hurt us in any way but to flip the ego's reality upside down, just to reorient points of reference into the soul's perspective.

Each and every time the grace of devastation enters our reality, we have an equal opportunity to either cement the falsehood of limiting beliefs or to allow limiting beliefs to melt away by walking through the fire of our most epic disaster.

We may not know why things are happening or where it's all going, but in order for the soul to lead the way, the ego must be shaken from its grip of control. The more we are willing to align with Source, trust in the gift of our journey, and welcome devastation without requiring difficulty in order to grow, the easier all aspects of life transform from the inside out.

From this space, we develop long-lasting sacred partnerships in which two people can merge and harmonize with each other, without constant emotional triggers, limiting beliefs, or patterns of conditioning dividing one heart from the other.

STAGE 5: EMBRACING ADVERSITY

As we discover the freedom to meet each other as expressions of our own divinity, we find the safety, comfort, and courage to remain open, even when pain or panic are begging us to run away, withdraw, check out, or shut down.

When everything is here to help you, despite how callous, unbearable, and insufferable life seems, the most unwavering faith to our deepest truth *always* leads us home, no matter how displaced we may be for any amount of time. From the viewpoint of ego, the plight of adversity confirms that since things don't seem okay, they can only continue to not be okay. Only the ego says no to the pain and despair of unavoidable loss.

And yet, from the soul's perspective, nothing is required to feel or be in any other way than how it unfolds. This is because the soul is the inherent trust existing within the oneness of Source energy that becomes more of an instinctive experience as your journey of surrender deepens.

While the truth of Source energy is ever present and eternal, any tangible form, including the ego, can only exist in a dimension of time. If it exists in time, it's always bound to change. No pain or loss can truly last forever, but in whatever way is needed for it to let go it will be relentless in the ego's unraveling.

To clarify another outdated belief of the old spiritual paradigm, you are not the one who lets things go. You are the one who *is let go of.*

Once the ego is dissolved by the unavoidable winds of change, a renewed space welcomes into our reality fresh experiences and greater perspective.

To step forward into the forefront of the soul's journey, it is essential to take the next leap into stage five of our deepest heartfelt surrender. It can be accessed by considering the following question:

How can I view adversity in a way that is more loving, supportive, and wise?

Simply by considering this option, we are aligning with the soul by serving the needs of our experience. Once we recognize the limiting beliefs that have kept us so stuck, we can use the power of our ever-expanding awareness to consider viewpoints that support our innocent nature rather than undermine it.

In order to embrace adversity as an entry point into stage five of surrender, please consider the wisdom of the following questions:

What is life like when everything is reward without belief in punishment?

Is life really punishing me or just not giving me what I want?

What if not getting what I want for a temporary amount of time is a gift in disguise?

What if my struggles transformed relationships and realities, creating higher levels of intimacy and fulfillment?

What qualities are being refined when adversity occurs?

Is it possible that I'm only meant to survive each adversity to help me see myself in all my magnificence, power, and glory?

As we end the plight of personal abandonment and allow the grip of attachment to dissolve, we dare to meet each moment beyond the framework of limiting beliefs, no matter how much devastation or adversity we are meant to face. From this space, we allow the old paradigm of reality to be set ablaze, so the inner phoenix of our true angelic potential can triumphantly ascend from its ashes.

To help embody the insights of the five stages of surrender, please consider the wisdom of or repeat aloud the following statement:

I accept that my transition from ego to soul occurs through my deepest heartfelt surrender. Instead of blaming each circumstance and character for the expansions they inspire, I relinquish each weapon of defense, so I may embrace how everything is here to help me.

This occurs by seeing each moment in a way that helps instead of hurts me, finding the courage to admit what I am afraid to admit, lose, or gain, considering how the worst things that ever happened to me were the greatest opportunities to evolve and embrace my deepest truth even if it means being devastated, while viewing each moment of change in the most loving, supportive, and wise way.

From this space of heartfelt surrender, I am able to honor things as unique expressions of Source energy, where life can ebb and flow without shaking my sense of self-worth. As this occurs, I am elevating my vibration, as well as uplifting the consciousness of humanity for the well-being of all. And so I am released.

Whether we are feeling more relief, inner peace, and harmony than ever before, or still making our way through the integration of each stage, it is our willingness to surrender to life on its precise terms and conditions that manifests the beauty, power, and perfection of our highest potential. Maybe there appears to be a brighter light at the end of the tunnel, or maybe there is just too much darkness for one person to bare. In either case, there always remains a deeper reason for why things happen for the fulfillment of a mission that you incarnated to complete.

CHAPTER 8

FULFILLING
YOUR
MISSION

As we make our way through the five stages of surrender, we are able to experience the miraculous depths of our journey from the soul's perspective. As we surrender to a bigger cosmic picture, we begin to find our lifelong place in the cosmos as a living expression of Source energy that incarnated to fulfill an important mission. Such a mission entails the completion of our healing journey as our personal contribution toward shifting the collective consciousness of humanity. While it may seem as if we are merely one person on a singular personal journey, the themes we face and the conflicts we ultimately resolve become the very gifts of renewed freedom the world receives in our presence. In essence, what we are healing in *ourselves*, we are helping to transform in *all*. Equally so, the layers of emotional debris we've already healed become the exact themes that others can transform when around us.

Perhaps more rooted in love than ever before, we can further participate in the awakening of humanity by inviting the miraculous grace of Source energy to further assist in our healing. While many yearn to skip past the initial phases of expansion by jumping right into the clearing of physical pain or emotional discomfort, the healing journey isn't always designed to work in that preferred order of operation. Once we are able to harmonize with the Universe on its precise terms and conditions, we cultivate a depth of maturity and readiness to invite such resolution to unfold.

As stated in earlier chapters, the very symptoms that many hope for a spiritual journey to resolve are often the very evidence of healing under way. This means each moment of pain or layer of discomfort is a sign of energetic and emotional change already in progress. When we trust that the Universe is always transforming us into the destiny of our highest Divine perfection, we can ease into harmony with our healing journey, instead of working so hard to micromanage our experiences.

Each experience is designed to help us expand in the most efficient span of time. If it were to occur more slowly, it would take so much longer to make our way through the difficult chapters of evolution, which would create longer durations of suffering to endure.

THE FOUR SIGNS OF TRANSFORMATION

Because Source energy is all-knowing and all-loving, it yearns to move us through each stage of growth and expansion in the most effective way. When transformation occurs rapidly, such change can be noticed as one of four palpable signs. Each one acts as a confirmation that our healing is well under way, as the grace of reality moves us through each stage as efficiently as we allow it to unfold.

The four signs of transformation are frustration, confusion, boredom, and loneliness. While each of these signs assists the soul in realizing how powerful a journey is occurring from the inside out, each one equally represents the experiences that ego attempts to deny or use a spiritual journey to transcend. True transcendence is seeing evolution through to completion, while making peace with the frustration, confusion, boredom, and loneliness that merely confirm how rapidly we are expanding.

To embrace each of the four signs of transformation, please consider the wisdom of the following questions:

What if frustration, confusion, boredom, and loneliness are not barriers at all?

What if such feelings are only enemies to an unraveling ego?

What if each feeling is only as overwhelming or debilitating as my desire to turn away from discomfort?

How do frustration, confusion, boredom, and loneliness change if I welcome them as allies of evolution?

What if, in addition to acting as signs of transformation, it's not my personal frustration, confusion, boredom, and loneliness I am experiencing, but the patterns of humanity I'm healing for all?

BEYOND PERSONAL OWNERSHIP

While the ego often views healing as a personal punishment to resolve or a hardship to endure, the soul views the expansion of the individual as a contribution toward transforming the collective. If every experience we heal in ourselves acts as a layer of emotional debris transmuted throughout the world, then perhaps the conditioning being healed was never ours to begin with.

From the viewpoint of ego, every facet of experience maintains a framework of identity and ownership. As long as experiences are owned and identified as *ours* versus *theirs*, we stay divided from Source, unable to heal the wounds that inspire our light to shine. The truth is, we are having personal experiences for the purposes of unearthing our never-ending expansion and to transform the world in view. As stated in earlier chapters, there only appears to be a world in need of healing, as an interactive curriculum for angels in training.

The more the soul expands, the more angelic we become as we advance throughout each stage of mastery along our human adventure.

The more time we spend rooted in the wisdom of the soul, the more our earthly realm appears to be an angelic university existing in heaven. But when we are incubating in ego, Earth tends to feel like a lower-level existence, as we reach toward the sky waiting to be rescued by an elusive higher power.

As we continue to shift from ego to soul, we graduate into higher levels of angelic training by transforming the plight of the planet through the power of heart-centered consciousness. We do this by relinquishing our attachments to owning and identifying with experiences, so we are able to heal the very themes that inspire the world to awaken.

While there is no denying the reality of our personal experiences, they exist as opportunities to clear space in our energy fields—as a way of inviting a greater spiritual reality to emerge.

A NEW LOOK AT KARMA

What if moments of adversity are not our personal karma, but the aspect of the collective we are transforming for the well-being of all?

What if the notion of personal karma were simply an unconscious tendency to identify with the layers of emotional debris our energy fields transmute in all we encounter?

What if our current symptoms, illness, or patterns of conditioning are the very layers we are healing for the benefit of future generations?

What if the awareness that nothing we feel has anything to do with us is how we clear the karma of humanity that has been held in our energy fields until this realization dawns?

The moment we open to the possibility that adverse experiences are not ours, but a contribution toward a more evolved humanity, we begin to lighten the load of our energy field. From this space of clarity, we are able to release what was never evidence of who we are or aren't, so we may welcome the joy of liberation far before the collective reflects it back.

The collective shifts as a result of a tipping point in consciousness. As our lifetime of healing is honored as a contribution toward tipping the collective scales into higher vibrations, we can continue to uplift those around us without being weighed down by their emotional density.

When what we feel is not ours to control, but an ongoing opportunity to clear out global density, we become the first residents of our newly upgraded reality. As this unfolds, we freely and effortlessly shine our light in every direction to assist other innocent hearts in finding their way home.

The more we become aware of our energy field as a healing and activation catalyst, the more we align with Source to integrate the brightness of our soul into physical form. When identifying with "my pain" or "my healing journey," the ego remains stuck and insufferable as long as it remains attached to experiences through beliefs in personal ownership. However, when "my pain" becomes "humanity's pain" and "my healing journey" becomes "humanity's healing journey," a profound shift in consciousness occurs. From this space, we begin to sense the light of heaven in all things, merely taking shape and form as the exact experiences needed to advance us to the next level of angelic training.

EMPATHIC REINCARNATION

An empath is an energetically sensitive being who is aligned with their soul to the degree they are able to sense the emotions of others that their energy field clears. A victim is an empath in training, who equally clears and activates the energy fields of others but without the awareness of their living contribution to all.

No matter what world is perceived in view, it is made up of two distinct groups of empaths. There are those who know of their empathic tendencies but are left without a clue as to how to develop their innate gifts into fully functioning intuitive abilities. And there are also empaths who have no idea they are empathic and tend to see their journey through the eyes of blame and judgment.

When we are unaware of empathic abilities and energetic sensitivities, our energy field tends to take on the conditioning cleared in others by adding it on as additional layers to the fabric of our identity. The more we become aware of our empathic gifts, the more in harmony we are with our emotions as they arise, and the easier it is for us to clear each layer of emotional debris.

The more we align with the soul, the easier it is to uplift others without taking on their conditioning or acting out unconscious behavior.

The longer we stagnate in ego, the more likely we are to be overwhelmed by the world that only our evolution can resolve.

This doesn't mean the world suffers because we still have much to heal. Instead, the more our healing is guided by the wisdom of the soul, the more the world awakens.

When we come to terms with life's empathic misunderstanding, our experiences shed new light on the notion of reincarnation. In the old paradigm, reincarnation is the belief that as souls we've lived out many lifetimes prior to our current incarnation. While it is true that a soul has and will live out many lifetimes of perspective, it tends to give the ego much to sift through, organize, and keep straight. Ultimately, it provides ammunition to judge ourselves and others from the actions of other lifetimes, as a way of justifying its most limiting beliefs and unconscious patterns of behavior.

While the soul doesn't deny the reality of reincarnation, it certainly sees it from a more expansive viewpoint. From this perspective, the evidence we experience as our own past lives is reexamining in consciousness the themes we incarnated to resolve for the world. If the ego adopts a spiritual identity, it is common to own the memories carried in our field as a road map of past pains and indiscretions. As a way of maintaining its unconscious state, if the ego isn't fed by its current personal identity, it is common for it to look to other lifetimes for more experiences to own.

Because we are ALL ONE, the memories we are clearing for countless lineages and generations tend to feel like they happened to us whenever they bubble up in our experience. Our memories may even include visions of experiences from other time periods, making us feel as if we were there. That's not to say we weren't there, since the moment such memories surface, we are experiencing it as if we were.

The transformation that occurs in real time, through the recalling of the past, is our ability to remember the visceral memories we are holding in our energy field. As each memory surfaces in consciousness without getting caught in the gravitational pull of identity, it is cleared out of our field for the well-being of humanity.

The question remains: Are we clearing out memories because we are healing what *actually* happened to us in past lifetimes, or does it only *feel* like previous incarnations, as we resolve the memories of past lineages for the evolution of the whole? While this can be widely debated, the answer comes in examining which viewpoint maintains an ego structure and which one aligns with the heart-centered consciousness of the soul.

It is not wrong to know past lives and even glean the wisdom from the archetypes and storylines each memory contains. However, it is very easy for the ego to claim ownership of such visions to enhance and expand its identity structure. Because the soul is a willing participant in the evolution of humanity, it can honor how meaningful each past life feels and even embrace the notion that each memory is a direct view into the mysteries of the past. Equally so, as each memory gets resolved, we are able to move forward without needing to drag any baggage along. From the soul's perspective, attachments to past lives are evidence that healing remains incomplete. Of course, healing occurs through the integration of ego. Therefore, trying to heal our personal past lives maintains the object of memory for ego to own.

When we approach healing in this counterproductive manner, we are feeding the very ego structure that needs to be unraveled. Because our point of view determines whether we spend more time building the ego or aligning with the soul, the power rests in our hands to assist in the timeless deconstruction of our most limiting experiences.

To allow the notion of past lives to unravel ego and align with the perfection of the soul, please consider the wisdom of the following questions:

What if I can learn from the past without believing that it happened to me personally?

What if it only feels like it happened to me, so that I can have a personal experience of the patterns I am resolving for all?

Instead of focusing on the storyline of each lifetime, what are the themes the character is learning throughout each vision?

What newly inspired choices can I begin making in my current reality that such characters weren't able to make in the past?

How can I resolve the past by learning to choose from a more courageous and conscious perspective, instead of using each memory to build a case against myself, others, or even Source?

As we evolve from the soul's perspective, we are able to make the most of our current lifetime while enjoying the gifts of experience that come our way. Whether arising as memories from distant civilizations or messages sent from a galactic neighbor light-years away, each and every experience offers us a deeper look into the immaculate artistry and infinite capacity of our consciousness that takes shape and form as endless worlds to explore.

To see a bigger cosmic picture is to be aware of the purity of our contribution, even if it requires an entire lifetime to notice, acknowledge, and accept. If we are unable to see beyond the viewpoint of personal struggles, we overlook the perfection of our existence, which confirms how all prayers are destined to be answered by the angelic light of incarnating souls. There is no denying that as souls we live out a multiplicity of experiences in many dimensions. Whether seeing them all playing out in simultaneous parallel universes or sensing their unfolding in linear order, it is essential to align with the insights that move us further into the perfection of the soul. This is not done to condemn or punish the ego, but to remove from its grasp the beliefs and viewpoints it uses to maintain self-fulfilling prophecies of perpetual suffering. Since we incarnated to return ego home to Source, each moment of realization and shifting of perspective must be embraced with the utmost grace and compassion. This allows the ego that senses its own demise to begin seeing it is actually being rescued by an openness that never excludes.

BORN FROM PERFECTION

If we were born from the source of perfection, then we were born *as* the perfection of Source. As our human qualities are embraced as expressions of divinity, we no longer see ourselves as wrestling with residues from past lives, but rather as healing memories for past lineages throughout the world. When each layer being cleared is not necessarily ours, we give permission to heal everything that we were born to resolve. No matter how deeply the ego insists, if we think each memory belongs to us, more time is given to validate such beliefs.

> **To remember the inherent perfection of our true nature, please consider the wisdom of the following questions:**
>
> *When was the first time I remember feeling less than Divine perfection?*
>
> *Did someone judge, criticize, or reject me into believing I was other than the beauty, power, and perfection of the Universe?*

Was there a time I shut down my light, hoping that being more like others would allow me to be better liked by others?

Am I able to accept that everything I adversely feel around others is a layer of debris my energy field is clearing out?

How would my life change if negative feelings were not inter-preted as mine or having anything to do with me, but rather as my contribution to an awakening humanity?

If we can mentally embrace the notion of being the per-fection of Source energy but can't seem to feel it within us, it is often because the emotions we clear out of others are still being used to maintain the identity of a lacking character.

Imagine a perfection that is so omnipresent, whole, and all-encompassing that in its oneness with all that is, there is no separation, distance, or conflict with anything in view.

In order to see a rainbow as the sum of all colors, one would need to set aside the notion of separate hues to see the full spectrum of beauty on display. In the same way, it is essential to set aside the idea of separation, including the dis-tinguishing characteristics of various thoughts and feelings, in order to sense the perfection within it all. When perfection is not a feeling to chase, but a comprehensive view of life's bigger cosmic picture, life can become easier and more en-joyable with each passing breath.

Since we would only attempt to resolve aggressively the things we believe are ours, the question remains: How many inner blockages or emotional enemies remain when remembering our role as life's eternal liberator, instead of someone waiting to be rescued? Such a question only fur-thers our alignment with Source energy in the most direct and heart-centered way.

THE SPIRAL STAIRCASE OF INSIGHT

Whether we believe our spiritual journey involves resolving karmic layers from past lives or clearing debris to help uplift the collective, it is common as healing deepens to notice recurring patterns surface.

Such patterns can be playing similar roles in relationships that mirror the conditioning of our family or acting out self-destructive habits when not fully aligned with Source energy.

No matter the patterns at play, when viewing our journey from the viewpoint of ego, it can be quite natural to want to speed through the healing process in hopes of getting to the other side of pain and misfortune. When this occurs, we are approaching the depths of spiritual maturity in a disingenuous way. This causes us to focus more on what we can get from the Universe, instead of living in authentic harmony with the flow of life.

Each moment should be savored as an opportunity to view our reality with renewed clarity, whether or not we wind up getting our way. When the learning curve of our ever-expanding nature can be embraced as a gift instead of perceived as a curse, we begin to see how abundant the Universe truly is.

Source already knows exactly who we are destined to become, which is why we came here to live out such a miraculous adventure. Source also knows our evolution was due to the inspired and courageous choices we made, as a result of the insights we've received. This is why we seem to repeat patterns and relationships, no matter how often we attempt to change the landscape of our reality. Source energy would never wish for anyone to miss a single morsel of wisdom or forget how pivotal a role each moment played in our triumphant redemption.

This is why things repeat for our benefit and never as a form of punishment. It allows the trajectory of our evolution to be much like a spiral staircase of insight. Just like when climbing up a spiral staircase, we may keep turning corners to see the same reality in view, but always see it from a higher perspective at each and every turn.

This means that even though patterns may repeat throughout our lives, we are always experiencing them from a more expanded level of consciousness than we had in the past. If we focus on experiences as superstitious forms of punishment, we innocently deny the consciousness within each moment that can see what has yet to be seen, while daring to respond as we have never responded before.

Because our primary shift in consciousness is transforming our relationship with reality, patterns and themes need to be seen from all angles and explored on a multitude of levels. While it seems as if we repeat the same patterns in life, we are actually turning the same corners in experience but from higher planes of perspective. This can free us from believing we'll be beyond each lesson once we get things right, so we may embrace the process that only ensures our most triumphant victory.

To help transform the soul's journey from spiritual punishment to evolutionary process, please consider the wisdom of the following questions:

What if each moment is more centered in learning, growing, and expanding than in trying to do everything right?

What if repeating patterns is life's way of helping me, instead of punishing me in any way?

What if everything I wish, need, want, and desire is already destined to arrive at exactly the moment it is meant to be?

What if this were true, whether or not I am able to trust such wisdom?

How would my life change if each moment were an evolutionary gift to receive, instead of a karmic punishment to escape?

How can each moment be seen from higher levels of consciousness, even when themes, patterns, characters, and outcomes seem to repeat?

The irony of heart-centered consciousness is in noticing how much maturity, integrity, and authenticity is required in order for your highest maturity, integrity, and authenticity to dawn. This is why the ego's greatest contribution to our expansion is letting go and integrating back into Source.

While the ego tries as desperately as possible to get everything right, it faces recurring moments of failure to inspire the greatest spiritual successes that always exist in the ego's absence. As our evolving consciousness becomes more rooted in our hearts, we are able to see how our mission is not getting rid of the ego. Instead, we are learning how to love the ego so unconditionally that it finds the safety and courage to let go and return to the light.

To help embody the insights of a bigger cosmic picture, please consider the wisdom of or repeat aloud the following statement:

I accept that I have incarnated to fulfill a mission that supports a bigger cosmic picture. This means I didn't necessarily come in with karmic patterns of indiscretions, but chose to carry imprints, conditioning, and cellular memory to heal familial lineages and to liberate humanity through my own healing. Since I was born from a loving Source of perfection, I could only be the perfection of a loving Source. In knowing it is so, I allow frustration, boredom, loneliness, and confusion to be embraced as signs of how rapidly I am expanding, rather than enemies to oppose, judge, or deny.

While patterns of experiences may repeat, I accept that this occurs for my evolutionary benefit, allowing me to see the same things from higher perspectives of consciousness each and every time. This helps me transform my view of life from spiritual punishment to evolutionary process, where everything is here to help me reach my absolute potential. And so I am fulfilled.

As the first section of our journey reaches a point of completion, we further align with Source energy by inviting the infinite miracles of the Universe to support our most triumphant transformation. As we each take steps forward into the light of our long-awaited destiny, we individually and collectively harmonize with the vibration of love that invites the world to awaken.

CLEARINGS, ACTIVATIONS & INTEGRATIONS

CHAPTER 9

CLEARINGS

AS OUR DEEPEST HEARTFELT surrender helps us cultivate the most mature and authentic alignment with Source, we invite the will of the Universe to demonstrate its immaculate capacity by healing our body and transforming reality in miraculous ways. While the very ego that often wants to be healed so desperately is actually the thing being resolved, there remain opportunities to expand at an accelerated rate, once we are living in harmony with the grace of our highest truth.

In Chapter 1, we examined how consciousness evolves through the equation of ARE. Since awareness combined with resolution creates the expansion of our soul, this next section of the book explores resolution on an energetic level. While it certainly has the potential to positively affect your physical, emotional, and energetic realities, it is always essential to engage with each tool from the wisdom of the soul's perspective. This means that while we may desire a specific type of healing, we surrender to the will of Source that in its infinite wisdom and unconditional love always knows exactly the depth of transformation that is needed.

Whether we feel strong or subtle responses to each clearing or activation, it does not indicate anything other than the gifts that are ready to be received. The ego wants what it wants, and it will stop at nothing to apply each tool or modality with as much aggression and repetition as necessary to create a desired outcome. Meanwhile, our soul lives in harmony with Source, grateful for the opportunity to experience each tool of expansion by simply following each step and allowing the magic to unfold.

As we explored in Chapter 5, healing isn't just a matter of what happens the moment a process is applied. It is more so rooted in how much of a healing can be absorbed throughout the integration process. While the goal is always to feel instantly lighter, happier, and more liberated than ever before, if a healing requires time to rest in order to be received, we may experience moments of exhaustion versus elation. Even when the positive feelings of a healing seem to fade away, it is merely the contrast of a new experience integrating into our energy fields to become a part of who we are, instead of an experience to track and manage.

Because integration plays such a pivotal role in the healing process, repeating each clearing and activation on a daily basis will not increase its potency. If anything, doing so has the potential to diminish the power of each process, since the strongest suggestion of clearing and activation occurs when accompanied by space to fully absorb each offering. Using each clearing and activation tool once every two weeks could enhance and benefit our evolution, but repeating each process more frequently suggests the conditioning of ego attempting to undermine the hands of time.

Each tool provided in this book has been offered at many of my five-day events, but I have never offered them in written or recorded form. Often referred to as "repeat after me" exercises, they have been channeled from Source and encoded with healing frequencies that positively affect our energy field and subconscious mind. Each "repeat after me" exercise can be read silently, although it tends to benefit the subconscious mind more when recited aloud. Oftentimes, when reading each clearing and activation aloud, it is common for our minds to lose track of the words. This is due to our conscious mind settling into a state of lucid rest, while our subconscious mind is rewired by the energies encoded in the words. Just by repeating each clearing and activation, we energetically receive the benefit each healing provides, whether we blank out or remember what was said.

To assist in our soul's evolution, so we may further our angelic training and discover the true joy of liberated existence, I offer these tools as catalysts of transformation for the journey ahead. Because each tool was created in the light of heart-centered consciousness, the only energies we are able to receive from each process are the gifts of evolutionary benefit that our higher self, angels, and spirit guides allow us to receive.

With a relaxed mind and an open heart, we invite the magic and miracles of Source energy to reveal our highest potential in loving service for our long-awaited destiny and all the lives we came to uplift.

HEALING STARTS WITH INTENTION

**To begin the healing process of energetic clearing,
please repeat the following intention,
either silently or aloud:**

I intend for the following clearings to act as conduits of miraculous revelation, always providing the exact results that align with my highest truth. I accept that I am worthy of this healing and allow my consciousness to expand to create sacred space for my soul to reside. In knowing it is so, I allow any emotional debris, conditioning of ego, patterns of heredity, imprints from genetic lineages, and all energies that are not mine and do not belong to me to be cleared out of my energy field, returned to the Source of their origin, and transmuted completely—now and forever. From this moment forward, I embrace my mastery as a surrendered expression of heart-centered consciousness, living out my most triumphant redemption that completes my mission, transforms my reality, and liberates all by the immaculate power of Source energy. And so it is.

LIGHTENING UP YOUR ENERGY FIELD

This "repeat after me" process was channeled to clear attachments of ownership and dissolve patterns of ego throughout the human energy field. As it was channeled, the usage of the word *love* acknowledges the truth of Source energy in its fully awakened and embodied form.

**To lighten up your energy field, please read,
either silently or aloud, the following statements:**

*I acknowledge that no thought belongs to me, because I am the
love within it.*

*No feeling or reaction belongs to me, because I am the love
within it.*

No memory belongs to me, because I am the love within it.

*No conditioning or programming belongs to me, because I am
the love within it.*

*No lineage or pattern of heredity belongs to me, because I am
the love within it.*

*No illness, disease, or imbalance belongs to me, because I am
the love within it.*

*No tragedy, loss, or limitation belongs to me, because I am the
love within it.*

*No form of darkness, cruelty, or negativity belongs to me, be-
cause I am the love within it.*

*No form of pain, heartbreak, war, or conflict belongs to me,
because I am the love within it.*

*No form of insecurity, doubt, or poverty belongs to me, because
I am the love within it.*

*No form of separation belongs to me, because I am the love
within it.*

*No form of abandonment belongs to me, because I am the love
within it.*

*And since I am the love within all things, I allow all things that
are not of love—which can only be judgments imagined about
love—to be cleared out of my energy field; returned to the
Source of their origin, transmuted completely; returned to the
purity, wholeness, and perfection of eternal light; and reborn in
awakened, heart-centered consciousness as the love that I am.
And so it is.*

THE STARSEED CLEARING

This was channeled from the Universe in response to my intention to offer an interactive modality to help purify, activate, and awaken the light of Source energy throughout all aspects of the human energy field. While many beings have awakened various aspects of their energy field, many others are in need of synthesizing each part, so the totality of light in all can be integrated into a fully embodied expression of heart-centered consciousness.

The following process serves to clear, cleanse, and purify all aspects of our physical body to promote wellness on an emotional and energetic level.

Please read, either silently or aloud, the following clearings, pausing for two to three minutes in between sections to allow the healing energies to integrate, maximizing benefit and absorption:

I accept that all my organs have already been cleansed, cleared, and purified, manifesting the highest possibility of eternal light that I AM NOW. In knowing it is so, I welcome these creations into my present-moment reality, to be embodied at full capacity in the light of consciousness as the Holy Creator I AM. And so it is.

(Pause for two to three minutes.)

I accept that all my bodily systems have already been cleansed, cleared, and purified, manifesting the highest possibility of eternal light that I AM NOW. In knowing it is so, I welcome these creations into my present-moment reality, to be embodied at full capacity in the light of consciousness as the Holy Creator I AM. And so it is.

(Pause for two to three minutes.)

I accept that all my glands have already been cleansed, cleared, and purified, manifesting the highest possibility of eternal light that I AM NOW. In knowing it is so, I welcome these creations into my present-moment reality, to be embodied at full capacity in the light of consciousness as the Holy Creator I AM. And so it is.

(Pause for two to three minutes.)

I accept that all parts of my brain have already been cleansed, cleared, and purified, manifesting the highest possibility of eternal light that I AM NOW. In knowing it is so, I welcome these creations into my present-moment reality, to be embodied at full capacity in the light of consciousness as the Holy Creator I AM. And so it is.

(Pause for two to three minutes.)

I accept that all my hormones have already been cleansed, cleared, and purified, manifesting the highest possibility of eternal light that I AM NOW. In knowing it is so, I welcome these creations into my present-moment reality, to be embodied at full capacity in the light of consciousness as the Holy Creator I AM. And so it is.

(Pause for two to three minutes.)

I accept that all my neurotransmitters and aspects of metabolism have already been cleansed, cleared, and purified, manifesting the highest possibility of eternal light that I AM NOW. In knowing it is so, I welcome these creations into my present-moment reality, to be embodied at full capacity in the light of consciousness as the Holy Creator I AM. And so it is.

(Pause for two to three minutes.)

Whether you are feeling the immediate relief of these clearings or require time to rest and assimilate their effects, you are opening up doorways within you for the evolution of your soul and the well-being of all. With time as an ally instead of an enemy, the benefits of these clearings as well as the healing work done throughout the course of many lifetimes begin to surface into tangible form.

CHAPTER 10

ACTIVATIONS

The following process is known as the Starseed Activation. It serves to activate and awaken heart-centered consciousness throughout all aspects of the physical body.

THE STARSEED ACTIVATION

To invite the awakening benefits of the Starseed Activation, please read, either silently or aloud, the following activations, pausing for two to three minutes in between sections to allow the healing energies to integrate, maximizing benefit and absorption:

I accept that all my organs have already been activated and awakened, manifesting the highest possibility of eternal light that I AM NOW. In knowing it is so, I welcome these creations into my present-moment reality, to be embodied at full capacity in the light of consciousness as the Holy Creator I AM. And so it is.

(Pause for two to three minutes.)

I accept that all my bodily systems have already been activated and awakened, manifesting the highest possibility of eternal light that I AM NOW. In knowing it is so, I welcome these creations into my present-moment reality, to be embodied at full capacity in the light of consciousness as the Holy Creator I AM. And so it is.

(Pause for two to three minutes.)

I accept that all my glands have already been activated and awakened, manifesting the highest possibility of eternal light that I AM NOW. In knowing it is so, I welcome these creations into my present-moment reality, to be embodied at full capacity in the light of consciousness as the Holy Creator I AM. And so it is.

(Pause for two to three minutes.)

I accept that all parts of my brain have already been activated and awakened, manifesting the highest possibility of eternal light that I AM NOW. In knowing it is so, I welcome these creations into my present-moment reality, to be embodied at full capacity in the light of consciousness as the Holy Creator I AM. And so it is.

(Pause for two to three minutes.)

I accept that all my hormones have already been activated and awakened, manifesting the highest possibility of eternal light that I AM NOW. In knowing it is so, I welcome these creations into my present-moment reality, to be embodied at full capacity in the light of consciousness as the Holy Creator I AM. And so it is.

(Pause for two to three minutes.)

I accept that all my neurotransmitters and aspects of metabolism have already been activated and awakened, manifesting the highest possibility of eternal light that I AM NOW. In knowing it is so, I welcome these creations into my present-moment reality, to be embodied at full capacity in the light of consciousness as the Holy Creator I AM. And so it is.

(Pause for two to three minutes.)

COMPLETING THE STARSEED ACTIVATION

**To allow the healing benefits of the Starseed Clearing
& Activation to be absorbed at their highest capacity,
please read the following statement,
either silently or aloud:**

*I allow all clearings, healings, and expansions of the Starseed
Activation to be cleansed, purified, activated, and awakened,
manifesting the highest possibility of eternal light that I AM NOW.
In knowing it is so, I welcome these creations into my
present-moment reality, to be embodied at full capacity in the
light of consciousness as the Holy Creator I AM. And so it is.*

THE ART OF BEING

This process was channeled to activate experiences of reality
beyond the realm of understanding. When the need for constant understanding is set aside, we relinquish attachments to
control—to be the truth of Source energy, instead of the one
attempting to track and manage it.

**To activate the Art of Being, please read the
following statements, either silently or aloud:**

I cannot understand innocence.
   I can only be the innocence that I AM.

I AM innocence; innocence I AM.

I cannot understand peace.
   I can only be the peace that I AM.

I AM peace; peace I AM.

I cannot understand joy. I can only be the joy that I AM.

I AM joy; joy I AM.

I cannot understand freedom.
I can only be the freedom that I AM.

I AM freedom; freedom I AM.

I cannot understand transcendence.
I can only be the transcendence that I AM.

I AM transcendence; transcendence I AM.

I cannot understand here. I can only be the here that I AM.

I AM here; here I AM.

I cannot understand light. I can only be the light that I AM.

I AM light; light I AM.

I cannot understand truth. I can only be the truth that I AM.

I AM truth; truth I AM.

I cannot understand the way.
I can only be the way that I AM.

I AM the way; the way I AM.

I cannot understand being.
I can only be the being that I AM.

I AM being; being I AM.

I cannot understand love. I can only be the love that I AM.

I AM love; love I AM.

I cannot understand all. I can only be the all that I AM.

I AM all; all I AM.

I cannot understand one. I can only be the one that I AM.

I AM one; one I AM.

With tremendous healing comes the necessity of integration. This reminds us to trust in the natural flow of our healing process with nothing to push against or rush along. If you happen to be feeling more open, spacious, or even happy, it is a sign that your integration process is already under way. If you feel empty, blank, or even numb, it is merely an indication that you are entering the integration phase, which contains a far subtler form of energy than our five basic senses are accustomed to noticing. To whatever degree your experience reflects, it could only be an indication of how uniquely you are destined to awaken, since everything is here to help you heal and transform.

CHAPTER 11

INTEGRATING
YOUR
EXPERIENCES

JUST AS IMPORTANT as each clearing and activation is the integration of our most transformative experiences. While insights may come in a flash as we activate, heal, and awaken, they need time to be assimilated, much like the period of time your body requires to digest a delicious meal. The more we embrace the importance of integrating, the more we can embody our soul's highest qualities—no matter the experiences of others or the state of the world.

INTEGRATING INTO EMPTINESS

This process was channeled to invite greater inner spaciousness to help integrate the healings, clearings, and activations that are received. The word *emptiness* was channeled to amplify the formless qualities of the soul to help further unravel the ego and embody the light of heart-centered consciousness.

To integrate into emptiness, please read the following statements, either silently or aloud:

All is emptiness; emptiness is all.
One is emptiness; emptiness is one.
None is emptiness; emptiness is none.
Space is emptiness; emptiness is space.
Sound is emptiness; emptiness is sound.

Name is emptiness; emptiness is name.
Form is emptiness; emptiness is form.
Time is emptiness; emptiness is time.
Nothing is emptiness; emptiness is nothing.
Everything is emptiness; emptiness is everything.

Thinking is emptiness; emptiness is thinking.
Feeling is emptiness; emptiness is feeling.
Moving is emptiness; emptiness is moving.
Still is emptiness; emptiness is still.
Perceiving is emptiness; emptiness is perceiving.

Noticing is emptiness; emptiness is noticing.
Aware is emptiness; emptiness is aware.

Breathing is emptiness; emptiness is breathing.
Living is emptiness; emptiness is living.
Learning is emptiness; emptiness is learning.

Discerning is emptiness; emptiness is discerning.
Growing is emptiness; emptiness is growing.
Opening is emptiness; emptiness is opening.
Awakening is emptiness; emptiness is awakening.
Realizing is emptiness; emptiness is realizing.

Liberating is emptiness; emptiness is liberating.
Being is emptiness; emptiness is being.
Knowing is emptiness; emptiness is knowing.
Everything is emptiness; emptiness is everything.
Nothing is emptiness; emptiness is nothing.

Time is emptiness; emptiness is time.
Form is emptiness; emptiness is form.
Name is emptiness; emptiness is name.
Sound is emptiness; emptiness is sound.
Space is emptiness; emptiness is space.

None is emptiness; emptiness is none.
One is emptiness; emptiness is one.
All is emptiness; emptiness is all.

BEING YOURSELF - PART ONE

This two-part process was channeled to further the integration process by moving beyond the play of opposites to reside in our natural state of heart-centered consciousness.

Although the ego can have fears of using words to renounce positive states, it is a process that cannot take away all the goodness we are meant to receive. Instead, it is a way of using the power of words to rest as the ocean of existence, instead of being tossed back and forth between the waves of pleasure and pain.

Despite how superstitious the ego tends to be, nothing but the utmost peace, ease, integration, and absorption of healing energy can manifest as a result of this "repeat after me" exercise.

In Part One, the words *you* and *yourself* were channeled to loosen attachments to external perceptions of opposites. The more rooted we are in being ourselves, without the boundary of symbols or definitions, the easier it is to be in the world and meet others in the most peaceful, empowered, and loving way.

To integrate all clearings and activations by being yourself at a more undefined level, please read the following statements, either silently or aloud:

You're not right. You're not wrong. You're just being yourself.
You're not different. You're not similar. You're just being yourself.
You're not here. You're not there. You're just being yourself.
You're not in time. You're not out of space.
    You're just being yourself.
You're not lucid. You're not asleep. You're just being yourself.

You're not obedient. You're not resistant.
    You're just being yourself.
You're not motivated. You're not depressed.
    You're just being yourself.
You're not certain. You're not uncertain.
    You're just being yourself.
You're not a victim. You're not a villain.
    You're just being yourself.
You're not passive. You're not angry. You're just being yourself.

You're not excited. You're not sad. You're just being yourself.
You're not unsure. You're not confused. You're just being yourself.
You're not greedy. You're not poor. You're just being yourself.
You're not constant. You're not changing. You're just being
    yourself.
You're not hopeful. You're not hurting. You're just being yourself.

You're not paroled. You're not imprisoned. You're just being yourself.
You're not included. You're not excluded. You're just being yourself.
You're not satisfied. You're not starving. You're just being yourself.
You're not formed. You're not unformed. You're just being yourself.
You're not known. You're not unknown. You're just being yourself.

You're not in focus. You're not out of reach. You're just being yourself.
You're not like anything. You're not unlike anything.
    You're just being yourself.
You're not cause. You're not effect. You're just being yourself.
You're not before anything. You're not beyond anything.
    You're just being yourself.
You're not me. You're not you. You're just being yourself.

You're not coming. You're not going. You're just being yourself.
You're not this. You're not that. You're just being yourself.
You're not relative. You're not absolute. You're just being yourself.
You're not fact. You're not falsehood. You're just being yourself.
You're not what if. You're not what isn't. You're just being yourself.

You're not deniable. You're not understandable.
    You're just being yourself.
You're not lost. You're not found. You're just being yourself.
You're not visible. You're not invisible. You're just being yourself.
You're not imagined. You're not unreal. You're just being yourself.

BEING YOURSELF – PART TWO

In Part Two the words *I* and *myself* are channeled to free us from attachments to internal symbols and definitions. The more undefined we allow ourselves to be, the more our experiences can expand.

**To integrate all clearings and activations by being
yourself at a more undefined level, please read the
following statements, either silently or aloud:**

I'm not right. I'm not wrong. I'm just being myself.
I'm not different. I'm not similar. I'm just being myself.
I'm not here. I'm not there. I'm just being myself.
I'm not in time. I'm not out of space. I'm just being myself.
I'm not lucid. I'm not asleep. I'm just being myself.

I'm not obedient. I'm not resistant. I'm just being myself.
I'm not motivated. I'm not depressed. I'm just being myself.
I'm not certain. I'm not uncertain. I'm just being myself.
I'm not a victim. I'm not an enemy. I'm just being myself.
I'm not passive. I'm not angry. I'm just being myself.

I'm not excited. I'm not sad. I'm just being myself.
I'm not certain. I'm not confused. I'm just being myself.
I'm not greedy. I'm not poor. I'm just being myself.
I'm not constant. I'm not changing. I'm just being myself.
I'm not hopeful. I'm not hurting. I'm just being myself.

I'm not paroled. I'm not imprisoned. I'm just being myself.
I'm not included. I'm not excluded. I'm just being myself.
I'm not satisfied. I'm not starving. I'm just being myself.
I'm not formed. I'm not unformed. I'm just being myself.
I'm not known. I'm not unknown. I'm just being myself.

I'm not in focus. I'm not out of reach. I'm just being myself.
I'm not like anything. I'm not unlike anything.
    I'm just being myself.
I'm not cause. I'm not effect. I'm just being myself.
I'm not before anything. I'm not beyond anything.
    I'm just being myself.

I'm not me. I'm not you. I'm just being myself.

I'm not coming. I'm not going. I'm just being myself.
I'm not this. I'm not that. I'm just being myself.
I'm not fact. I'm not falsehood. I'm just being myself.
I'm not what if. I'm not what isn't. I'm just being myself.
I'm not deniable. I'm not understandable. I'm just being myself.

I'm not lost. I'm not found. I'm just being myself.
I'm not visible. I'm not invisible. I'm just being myself.
I'm not imagined. I'm not unreal. I'm just being myself.

As time offers us the gift of integration, we are able to be ourselves at full capacity, whether or not we are able to fathom or comprehend the truth of our miraculous nature. Once we have settled into ourselves, a deeper purpose for our existence can be known that equally unites us as one, while embracing the uniqueness of our individual expression.

CREATING
A NEW
REALITY

CHAPTER 12

WHY
WE ARE
HERE

AS WE HAVE BEEN EXPLORING up to this point, we are here on this planet to further our angelic training as an awakening soul in physical form. We were placed in a family structure during our earliest and most impressionable years of development as a microcosmic model of the collective consciousness that we incarnated to help shift.

In preparation for our spiritual journey, we replicated cellular memories and patterns of behavior modeled by those around us. This began the incubation phase within the cocoon of ego as a foreshadowing of inevitable and greater expansion. By surviving each and every experience that came our way, our ego was shaped into the very character through which the light of Source energy would enter as a fully embodied soul.

Whether plagued by hardship, devastated by loss, ambushed by rejection, or overwhelmed by adversity, each chapter of our adventure has served to expand our consciousness and refine our perceptions as activators of evolution. Our journey isn't just a means of becoming a greater expression of Source energy but of returning to the perfection that we knew ourselves to be before this lifetime began.

From incubating ego to embodied soul, the vibration of heart-centered consciousness grows and extends throughout every layer of our energy field. When all layers have been filled up, such expansive energy has nowhere else to go but to pour outside of our field and fill up every form we perceive as the world in view. As our ability to expand uplifts the consciousness of the planet and accelerates the healing of others, the outside world begins to confirm the arrival of our mastery by reflecting back the amplified energy that we have been radiating for all.

This doesn't mean we must wait until the world is awakened in order to embrace the destiny of the soul's completion. Instead, we are expanding our consciousness by embracing the RAW qualities of our soul's attributes to develop the ability to shine our light, instead of matching and mirroring the unresolved darkness that remains to be healed. By cultivating the four foundations of self-love and exploring the five stages of surrender, our inner polarity of energies are balanced out; so, we are able to be as loving and grounded as we are vast and wise. From this space, we are able to embrace the true intimacy of relationships as the living fulfillment of sacred partnership.

As alignment with Source manifests as our most noble actions toward ourselves and others, each personal interaction or seemingly inconsequential encounter becomes an opportunity to anchor more heart-centered consciousness.

Whether offering compliments on a more consistent basis, taking the time to embrace our own heart with greater authenticity, or even offering space to those who are too overwhelmed by their healing journey to respect the light we shine, each and every empowered choice raises the vibration of our inner experience to uplift the sum of the whole.

No matter how many times each pattern, role, or outcome resurfaces, it is always being seen from a higher perspective when accepting the terms and conditions of life as an evolutionary process instead of a personal punishment.

As pioneers of a new spiritual paradigm, we have entered the atmosphere of this planet to help dissolve every perceivable boundary dividing self from Source to allow all inhabitants of Earth to remember the heaven that always remains.

We are here because we are essential to the success of a mission that can only unfold as the perfection of destiny at play. We are here because we matter, and we matter because we've existed to be. The more we begin to matter to ourselves, the more the well-being of others can matter to us. As we honor how equally everything matters, the brightness of the soul moves fully into the tangibility of physical form to reconstruct reality from the highest vibration of truth.

This is our journey, and it is our mission together as ONE. Since each heart completes the ever-evolving destiny of Source energy, no matter the characters any of us play out, it confirms the absolute law of love that openness never excludes.

EVERYTHING IS A GIFT

When everything is a gift, it is a means of opening to the insights that confirm our most remarkable moments of expansion. Since it is common for the ego to use such an insight as a subtle form of manipulation, hoping to "learn its lessons" as quickly as possible so it can move beyond discomfort, torment, frustration, or confusion, it's easy to discount the usefulness of such a statement. When everything is a gift, it doesn't become the mantra suggested to someone in pain. Instead, we allow the presence of their despair, no matter how uncomfortable it may feel, to deepen our capacity to love for as long as our hearts can withstand it. In the new spiritual paradigm, we are not attempting to give anyone a better way of seeing anything. Instead, we remain grateful for the opportunities to meet in ourselves the feelings others instigate and embrace in others the struggles that carve out our highest rebirth along life's eternal road of redemption.

When everything is a gift, we are not trying to be anything other than fully available to however life seems to be. We remain open to the fact that everything exists to inspire the gifts of evolutionary benefit, whether noticed immediately or revealed over time.

When everything is a gift, we are open to the journey of evolution. We are willing to face any amount of adversity and spend as much time feeling shut down, just to cultivate the strength, courage, tenacity, and compassion to open back up more radiant, renewed, purified, and powerful than ever before. We acknowledge life's bigger cosmic picture without denying the grit and gravity of our feelings that signify how deep of a reconstruction is well under way.

When everything is a gift, we are not telling people how to experience their reality in any type of spiritually dogmatic way. We are honoring the relationship of opposites that flow throughout the oneness of truth. If one seems steeped in denial, it can only build up momentum to inspire an ability to face reality with greater authenticity, once such a shift is meant to occur. While sadness foreshadows the arrival of joy, and fear reflects a journey only guiding you into greater courage, it is not a transition that can be asserted with the insistence of ego.

Since the ego cannot force pain to become more pleasurable, it equally cannot get in the way of the perfection of our expansion. To ask ourselves, "How are we in our own way?" is to deny the way we've come to be, which will unearth a multitude of benefits at exactly the moment they are meant to occur.

Even if we are unable to fathom certain experiences as gifts, each circumstance or outcome merely confirms crucial stages of healing, where we must burn in the authenticity of our direct experience, simply to make more room for greater perspectives to dawn.

Nothing occurs because we lack perspective. Each experience ushers in a depth of awareness that could only help cultivate the brightness of light with time spent wandering in darkness.

When everything is a gift, we are not using light to diminish darkness but recognizing light as the capacity through which darkness is able to be acknowledged. Since darkness can be seen as consciousness unaware of its true illuminated nature, we allow the light of unconditional love to support, honor, and cherish darkness throughout its journey, without needing to rush the process.

To alter someone's experience is much like continually moving the seeds planted, hoping to find a more ideal spot for growth. Each time a seed is moved, the growing process is interrupted and disturbs the roots that are meant to sprout along their own rhythm of time.

While we don't wish to interfere with the energetic transformations occurring throughout each moment of healing, it doesn't mean we don't have valuable gifts to contribute.

Those who hurt are engaging in a healing process that will allow them to be the love, strength, courage, and compassion for others who heal. Those who have been healed have survived the perfect mixture of change, realization, and discovery, coming out the other side more aligned in their highest potential for the benefit of those still finding their way.

When everything is a gift, we are thankful for the sincerity of every person's living testimony and, daring to embrace the heart of another, grateful for the chance to meet aspects of our own eternal being. If we are unable to meet others in such a naturally open way, it could only remind us of the necessity of our own emotional needs. When this occurs, our hearts remain first in line to receive the infinite depth of unwavering attention that nourishes our innocence as it dares to transform.

When everything is a gift, there are highs, lows, and everything in between, giving us the chance to respond to life with more faith, respect, humility, kindness, and care under the threat of any circumstance.

When everything is a gift, we don't need to turn away from the hardships of reality in order to know the joy of faith. Equally so, there is no need to look for despair and pain to ensure you aren't missing or avoiding something. There is a middle ground. It's as natural as clearing enough space in our reality to notice the experiences we are already having.

Such a middle ground welcomes each experience openly, even if it means being open to feeling shut down for any amount of time.

In awakened, fully integrated, heart-centered consciousness, we are open to everything being a gift of evolution, whether we appreciate the conduct of others, agree with the situations in view, or wish such growth could occur under more favorable conditions.

We love what arises in ourselves if we have developed such a capacity. If not, the love within our hearts shall manifest as the compassion of others, the light emanating from nature or the silence of Source energy pulsating as every breath. We know that everything is inherently designed to make us better than we have ever been before, which requires us to be true to our journey, no matter how deeply we desire to speed things up or slow things down.

In the new spiritual paradigm, we value the gift of our most loving responses to life, despite how reactive we are to anything in view. If we are unable to respond from our hearts, more space, rest, and renewal is required to offer ourselves the nurturing attention seemingly absent in the behavior of others.

No one deserves to suffer for any reason, and we are not to blame for the experiences at hand. We have been given an opportunity to evolve, if we stay the course, which inevitably reveals an ability to expand without requiring adversity to inspire it. How do we get to such a destination? By being true to our feelings without projecting onto others and by embracing our own innocence, even when we seem to be the only ones who notice it.

When the response of our highest conduct outweighs the justification of any reaction, a surrendered heart is revealed. As we surrender, an abiding alignment with Source energy ushers in the beauty of heart-centered consciousness, no matter the amount of hurt that was seemingly required to reveal the glory of our perfection.

As we take each step with authenticity and compassion, it's not a gift until it's a gift. Once each gift is revealed, the benefits of its offering are awe-inspiring and infinitely magnificent.

CLARIFYING LIFE PURPOSE

In the old paradigm, life purpose was often imagined as a specific career, where the ego used spirituality as a form of reinvention. When and if this occurs, it is common to believe the dissatisfaction of a current profession is the reason for our unhappiness.

Sometimes there is truth in questioning whether we are living out our life's highest passion. If there is something else we yearn to do, we owe it to ourselves to move in that direction—no matter how intimidated we feel about the change we crave. At the same time, imagining life's highest purpose to be a spiritually oriented profession is where many are led astray.

If we are meant to earn a living through a spiritual profession, then opportunity will find its way to us before we even have a chance to pursue it. If a desire for a spiritual career isn't supported by the reality showing up, it is life's invitation to live a more spiritually fulfilling life no matter the name tag worn at a day job.

Life purpose isn't necessarily the role we play, but the specific way we choose to respond for the well-being of all. Often referred to as setting an intention, one of the most powerful ways to begin each day is by deciding how we wish to respond, no matter how anyone chooses to view or react to us.

Since everything is a gift, the clarity of life purpose is deciding the purpose of our existence by choosing the emotional offerings we wish to provide those we meet. When we are clear on the exact gifts we are open to sharing with others, the conviction of our generosity breaks the spell of energetically taking on other people's experiences.

When we have decided the exact gifts we wish to share, our consciousness becomes more rooted in receiving the gifts we offer, instead of taking on the emotional density our energy field heals in others.

A victim is not defined by the circumstances in view, but by how unaware they are of the gifts they were born to provide. A hero is not someone who never experiences fear, but one who doesn't allow doubts, concerns, and insecurities to hold them back from shining their light. As we shift from ego to soul, the inner victim transforms into the redeeming hero, as we live a life of greater purpose by doing things intentionally for the benefit of all.

Because ALL IS ONE, the gifts we consistently offer to others become the experiences perceived as life and the lens through which reality is viewed. Equally so, when we have not decided the gifts we were born to provide, a lack of intention translates into experiences of lack.

To clarify the question of life purpose, please consider the wisdom of the following questions:

What emotion do you wish for others to feel in your presence?

Is it the same emotion you yearn to feel more often?

What would your day be like if you were more focused on giving emotional gifts to others, instead of feeling what others withhold?

What if the best way to transform the collective victimhood of humanity is to make intentional choices that the world doesn't seem to make?

What if you only get pulled down by the energy of others or take on their conditioning by joining the world in withholding the gifts that reside within?

Once you decide the exact emotion that you wish for others to feel in your presence, which can also be the feeling you hope to experience more often, please clarify your life purpose by placing your chosen emotion in the blank space provided:

As a way of clarifying my life purpose, I intend to bless others with _____*, no matter how they choose to view or respond to me.*

The old "Fake it till you make it" scenario was employed to coerce the body into manufacturing more positive emotional states. But more often, we tend to feel the gifts we bestow upon others throughout each blessing. Notice how we don't have to feel specific emotions to bless someone with the exact feelings we wish for ourselves. Blessing is always an authentic act, from which we feel better about ourselves by focusing on the positive gifts we share.

Even if this feels like too big of a leap, it merely indicates a need to make you the central focus of your blessings. As anchors of heart-centered consciousness, the blessings offered to others uplift our own experiences, just as the blessings offered inward uplift the world around us. This is the miracle of unity.

THE ANATOMY OF A SMILE

One of the most powerful ways to transmit blessings is by smiling more often. A smile is an offering of goodwill. It is the spark of Divine energy between two people, pulling back the curtain of perception to remember the light dwelling in all. A smile is a subconscious ethical agreement; replacing the ways society may judge others as strangers with the openness of engagement, whenever eyes make direct contact. A smile is a celebration of our untainted innocent hearts, always ready and willing to burst with joy throughout moments of inspiration, no matter how broken down, beaten up, or defeated the past seems to be.

A smile is a declaration of freedom shining out from our eternally liberated nature, shouting passionately through the cosmic language of silence, "I am here. I matter. I exist for a reason." A smile is a gift of emotional generosity, like a gift certificate of healing energy, from which the receiver can decide where such energy can be best used for the evolution of their soul. A smile is a confirmation of alignment with Source and being settled in our highest truth, only revealing the need for deeper transformations the moment we look away, pull back, and hide.

A smile is a high five exchanged between angels affirming the perfection of their victory, despite how circumstances come to be. A smile is a remembrance of heaven sent from the purest space within us to awaken the purity of all. A smile is a symbol of awakened heart-centered consciousness affirming all that is whole, right, and perfect about this moment exactly as it is.

A smile is a spiritual cease-fire that only brings defeat to the parts and aspects that were never created to go any further.

A smile is a moment of profound surrender, no longer needing to hold anything together or manage a journey that is too busy taking care of you to brief you on its plan.

Whether as a gaze of ecstasy exchanged by lovers, the admiration given from parent to child, support sent from one friend to another, or an offering that bridges the borders between communities, may the remainder of life's journey be an opportunity to remember the power of our smile. If our smile seems to be lost, it is merely an opportunity to recognize the smiles of others, even when directed at others, as a way of getting back in touch with the joy that lives within us.

As we take the time to smile more deliberately, openly, and authentically, may we rejoice in how often we are given opportunities to positively interact with the unity of life, just by engaging in the simplest and sweetest acts of kindness more often. May we come to know our infinite wellspring of happiness that can be received with greater awareness the more often we open up and dare to shine.

EVERYTHING IS A CHOICE

As we cultivate heart-centered consciousness through the insights and practices of the new spiritual paradigm, we may find ourselves more aware of the choices at hand, without attempting to control the fate of every outcome. When the awareness of options outweighs a desire for control, our inherent freedom of being has been discovered.

From the perspective of ego, freedom is believed to be the effect of having leverage over reality. This is because the majority of painful moments were experienced as being controlled by reality in whatever way characters were created to affect our experience. One who has felt controlled by others often yearns to control others, simply as a way of escaping the potential of future pain and confinement. While the shift from victim to predator is common throughout the incubation of ego, as we expand from the soul's perspective, we are able to access the nature of true freedom without anything to impose, manipulate, or control.

THE VICTIM AND THE PREDATOR

The victim and predator act as the two basic archetypes of the ego. The victim represents the passive aspect, while the predator represents the aggressive side of human conditioning. Essentially, the movement of ego is various patterns of passive-aggressive behavior. It is the unconscious energy of passive-aggressive behavior that inspires the activities of worry, anticipation, and regret that also play out as responses of fight, flight, or freeze. Whether spending more time in one aspect or ping-ponging back and forth, the greater purpose of unconsciousness is to help build up emotional momentum to inspire an awakening of renewed perspective.

While there are many paths and approaches to waking up from the incubation of ego, it is common when not rooted in the most heart-centered approach to transform the victim into a spiritual victim and exchange the predator for a spiritual predator. This is why it is so essential to always remember how everything is here to help you. When life is on your side, even when appearing as characters that seem to undermine your radiance and joy, you are able to be in communion with the choices always available to you that no person, place, or thing can ever take away.

THE NATURE OF CONFLICT

The nature of conflict is a state of disharmony that occurs when some form of victimhood encounters any degree of predatory behavior. Even when victim encounters victim, the one more steeped in ego becomes the aggressive predator in the moment as the other cowers deeper into victimhood. The same occurs when predator meets predator. Inevitably, one asserts himself as the alpha of the moment, reducing the other predator to a more victimized role.

These are the painful patterns of human suffering that we as angels in training incarnated to dissolve and transmute for the well-being of all. Since ALL IS ONE, the choices made to cultivate the RAW qualities of our soul's highest attributes embrace the four pillars of self-love and complete the five stages of surrender helps you radiate an energy to awaken heart-centered consciousness throughout all corners of the globe.

ANCHORING A NEW SPIRITUAL PARADIGM

When the way we view each moment and how we choose to respond become our primary choices, we can valiantly step forward to fulfill our role as an anchor of a new spiritual paradigm.

Victimhood is a state of being affected by the choices of others, while refusing to consider the options at hand. Predatory behavior signifies feeling so shut down by the wounds of the past that we attempt to take away the choices of others to feel a depth of control that will never be found. Empowerment is recognizing how everything is here to help you make the most inspired heartfelt decisions that further your soul's expansion, despite how dastardly or disheartening any moment seems to be.

When rooted in heart-centered consciousness, everything is a choice. We may not have chosen the outcome, and we may find ourselves in an environment we dislike, but we always have choices and an ability to recognize the messages from Source that prompt us to become more honorable, courageous, thoughtful, and loving.

When people act lovingly in our presence, it is Source inviting us to cultivate higher frequencies of light by being just as loving to them, as well as to ourselves. When others are cruel, Source invites us to dive even deeper into self-love as a way of raising the vibration of the planet. While there is no evolutionary benefit to staying in abusive, emotionally toxic environments, we are always free to exit to a place of greater safety and help transform each victim and predator by loving ourselves.

According to the laws of unity consciousness, we don't actually have to share space with victims or predators in order to help unravel such patterns. Instead, we can merely take the time to treat ourselves and others better than we've ever been treated, whether communing with Source in public or embracing our hearts in private.

You may have believed that being abused meant there was something wrong with you that caused it to happen. Blaming yourself for the circumstances at hand can quickly lead to patterns of *spiritual* victimhood. The fact is, nothing is wrong with you. Instead, each moment is an opportunity to heal various patterns of the collective that play out as the ups and downs of your personal journey.

The more often we embrace the power of our choices in the most heart-centered way, the easier it is to help shift the collective without getting pulled into the gravity of its pain or assaulted by the unresolved healing in others.

The more that passive-aggressive patterns of victim and predator are returned to Source and integrated into the light of the soul, the more natural it is to see everything as an ally, even when disguised as an enemy. From this space, where everything is here to help you, you are the one helping everything transform simply by daring to make inspired choices.

ALL DIVINE, ALL HUMAN

Unity consciousness is the realization that ALL IS ONE. It is the governing force of the Universe expressing the absolute law of love throughout infinite space, recognizing that openness never excludes. When the truth of unity is fully embodied, the grace of heart-centered consciousness has been awakened. This occurs by integrating the ego into the soul to emerge as a self-actualized expression of Source energy. Instead of seeing it as exchanging personal experiences for a more spiritual-themed reality, try to view it as the arrival of our highest human potential—as the perfection of divinity in physical form.

This is why the mantra in the new paradigm is "All Divine, All Human." In essence, we are cultivating our highest cosmic attributes to manifest our purest and most fulfilling personal experiences. This is why human beings are not substandard expressions of Source energy, but rather opportunities for Source to express its immaculate perfection throughout the sensorium of time and space.

We are not a broken race aimlessly orbiting the solar system. We are the miraculous potential of life's eternal truth undergoing a radical global transformation through the healing and awakening of each individual.

We are becoming aware of ourselves as the grace of divinity in form. By simply daring to view ourselves and embrace our innocence the way Source always has, we may transform the world.

To know ourselves as truth is wisdom. To embrace that wisdom in ourselves as well as in others is the living reality of love.

As heart-centered consciousness is cultivated within and reflected throughout, more individuals are inspired to remember their true nature, just by being in the presence of those who dare to love. This is why we are here. It is our mission to fulfill throughout the unfolding of a destiny that guarantees we cannot get this wrong in any way.

We are all Divine, despite how we act or seem to be. We are all human, no matter how many spiritual insights we've collected along the way. We are born out of loving perfection, therefore we are only meant to return to the perfection of love, regardless of how imperfectly anything unfolds. Since everything is here to help you, anything you say or do must be helping the evolution of the whole. While such a statement isn't meant to justify cruel behavior or maintain self-destructive patterns, it helps to loosen your inner grip of control, so you can view life through the eyes of Source and remember the greatest purpose you are already living out.

MANIFESTING WITH LOVE

Since we are born from a Source of loving perfection, the perfection of our journey is returning to Source to manifest love as a tangible reality. As this occurs by integrating the ego from the soul's perspective, we are able to collaborate with Source energy to manifest our most incredible realities. Once we have completed the five stages of surrender and find ourselves naturally acting upon the four pillars of self-love more often than not, we gain access to miraculous new adventures that we are able to draw toward us through our journey in time.

While the Law of Attraction is typically taught as a means of getting what you want, the idea becomes remarkably simple and more emotionally supportive when you adopt a more heart-centered explanation for why things get attracted. If we've attracted adversity, it is only to disprove our most limiting beliefs by showing us the things we have the power to survive. Every single moment in time was created much like a hero's ever-expanding emotional arc in an epic saga.

When rooted in the soul's perspective, we are not as concerned with the things that happen but more so focused on how we respond to the situations in view. The Law of Attraction is here to remind us of the cosmic laws of Divine perfection, wherein everything occurs for a positive evolutionary benefit, even when viewed as life's worst-case scenario. It is not just an inspiring idea but a law of Universal Will, wherein anything and everything supports our highest expansion.

SPEAK YOUR TRUTH

Each moment is created to help us cultivate the highest qualities, most empowered responses, and radiant attributes of a fully awakened soul as our primary tool for transforming all aspects of life. Since we already are the truth of Source energy taking shape and form as the uniqueness of an individual, once fully surrendered, we can begin making requests in the name of love to allow the realities of our deepest desires to manifest.

Prior to surrender, it's easy to believe that we'll be the happiest when things outside of us change for the better. This is exactly why we don't have access to those powers. If so, we'd always be able to have what we wanted while stagnating at a level of consciousness that wouldn't allow us to feel worthy or be fulfilled by such desires. This is precisely why the initial stages of the spiritual journey are foundational. Once we've been energetically prepared to embody the frequency of light that supports the evolution of the planet, we are already rooted in the worthiness and consciousness to have what we want without giving away our power.

In the aftermath of learning how happy, whole, content, loving, peaceful, and free we can be, whether we get what we want or not, we have successfully stepped into an exciting new reality, where our desires can manifest as reflections of our ever-expanding vibration.

As we cultivate our soul's highest qualities by respecting, acknowledging, and welcoming each catalyst of spiritual growth, we can casually declare the things, events, resources, and outcomes that we would love—knowing so deeply in our hearts that we are only capable of drawing into our reality the desires that support our highest evolution. This is what it means to speak your truth. First we become the truth already dwelling within us, all so we can speak the truth of our heart's deepest desires, while fulfilling the desire of the Universe as angelic anchors of heart-centered consciousness.

In the new spiritual paradigm, the joy of asking for what you want and getting what you want measure the same on an energetic level. This means that every time we openly state a desire, we are acting as an advocate for our own innocence, allowing it to want freely what it wants without hesitation or restriction. It certainly doesn't mean we will always get what we want or that the things we desire are in our best interest to receive.

Because everything is here to help you, life is a matter of developing the worth to request the fulfillment of each desire, while allowing your highest wisdom to reveal exactly what you need to venture to your next highest level of consciousness. All too often, people aren't disempowered by their current circumstances but *stifled* by a depth of unworthiness that waits for desires to manifest, in order to feel safe enough to ask. Even when asking for what you want and not getting it, through the grace of a surrendered heart, you may discover a joy untouched by gains and losses that expands within you the more you speak your desires without attachment to outcome.

To cultivate the worthiness of speaking the truth of your heart's deepest desires, please consider the wisdom of the following questions:

What if asking for what we want brought joy faster than waiting to get what we want?

What if getting what we want cannot guarantee we will have the worthiness to fully receive it?

What if we always get what we want, but only at the moment it supports our highest evolution?

What if getting what we want at exactly the moment we're not ready to fully receive it is the worst-case scenario?

How can any moment of not getting what we want become an opportunity to embrace the wisdom of the Universe with greater faith, reverence, and respect?

What if waiting to get what we want were the best thing for us, no matter how desperate or deficient it may make us feel?

Perhaps more surrendered than ever before, you are able to see how asking for what you want allows you to feel equally empowered and supported, whether or not such creations come to be. From this space of renewed clarity, you are helping to transform reality for the well-being of all, simply by remembering that everything is here to help you.

To bring all the insights of this book together, please consider the wisdom of or repeat aloud the following statements from the book that have been woven together into one declaration of healing:

I accept the ego is the soul in its most dormant stages of incubation. It is not to be opposed, rejected, or denied, no matter how painful it may be when oscillating between patterns of worry, anticipation, and regret. I accept that I do not worry about, anticipate, or regret any of the reasons I may believe or have imagined.

I am simply playing out these patterns, as a way of building up momentum to inspire an awakening of consciousness. In knowing it is so, I allow all aspects of the inner WAR to be healed and resolved, as I create more space for my soul to expand. I embrace my most profound healing in the name of love, knowing all that I resolve within assists in transforming each heart throughout, since WE ARE ONE.

This helps me acknowledge that my spiritual journey is not a matter of dissecting myself under a spiritual microscope but rather allowing my soul's highest innate qualities to shine through more consistently and deliberately. This occurs by respecting the divinity in others, acknowledging the signs offered to best support each person's unique journey of healing, and welcoming the circumstances that inspire my most profound expansion, whether it matches my desires or not.

In knowing it is so, I allow all RAW qualities of the soul's highest attributes to be activated within and to radiate throughout for the well-being of all. From this moment forward, I am naturally rooted in the enthusiasm of each gift I am here to offer. I don't have to be afraid of what others may take from me or withhold from my heart.

There is a reason I am here. I exist with purpose. I came here to matter.

Having an open, receptive heart makes it easier to see how everything I experience is here to help me.

Whether representing patterns of emotional debris clearing out of my field or recognized as layers of unconsciousness healed throughout the collective, each thought and feeling is honored for its highest evolutionary benefit.

I embrace the nature of adversity that helps to create a proper melting point to transform personal rigidity into the light of my original form. I honor the gift of loss as it clears space in my reality for greater gifts to emerge. I acknowledge a deeper reason for fear as a signal from the Universe of impending growth. I respect the wisdom of anger that reveals when anyone is too overwhelmed by their healing journey to be able to interact in a heart-centered way. I welcome judgment as a helper who reminds me of the limiting beliefs I am clearing out of my energy field as well as that of others. I embrace the benefit of overthinking as an alarm clock informing me how open or closed my heart tends to be.

I recognize a deeper purpose for sadness as the very moment when the ego dissolves. I realize there is an upside to disappointment, as the ego is given further permission to unravel whenever it doesn't get its way. I recognize the prophetic power of jealousy as a foreshadowing of greater blessings entering my reality. I appreciate resentment as an unexpected liberator that shows me the areas of my life where I hold back from expressing my freedom of will at full capacity.

Instead of getting tangled up in the sounds of conflict, I can respect, honor, and welcome each spiritual ally through the power of my breath. In doing so, I serve my purpose as an angel in human form who incarnated to uplift the collective without having to dim my light or match the vibration of those around me.

With renewed clarity, I can see how resolution is not determined by bigger spiritual experiences but by allowing the subtlest of energies to be embraced by the highest vibration of consciousness already within me. This occurs by embracing the four foundations of self-love as a way of helping me integrate the healing journey already under way.

As I take the time to be well-rested, rooted in spaciousness, aligned with breath, and at peace with time, I deepen my own sacred partnership with myself. From this space, emotional receptivity becomes a gateway into transcendent spiritual experiences that come to me much faster than I can chase after them.

As this occurs, I am elevating my vibration as an announcer of well-being to inspire the world to be more caring and compassionate, just by taking time to nurture myself.

With greater enthusiasm, faith, and trust than ever before, I accept everything as a catalyst of spiritual evolution, no matter how inconvenient, painful, confusing, or frustrating it seems to be. Through the wisdom of the Golden Question, I allow the worst things that have ever happened to me to be embraced as the greatest opportunities I've been given to grow and evolve.

By separating the effect of my feelings from blaming the characters who seemed to cause them, I allow my emotions to be felt wholeheartedly, as a contribution toward my own healing journey, as well as the expansion of all. From this viewpoint of greater safety, I activate the power of true forgiveness by pardoning the characters in view and reminding myself that I wasn't the actual target of any attack. Instead, I am witnessing the many ways in which Source energy returns to its true nature throughout the awakening of every heart. This completes my first stage in the journey of surrender, which ushers me into an exciting new chapter of my journey, where there is everything to embrace and nothing to blame.

Perhaps I have incarnated to fulfill a mission that supports a bigger cosmic picture. What if I didn't necessarily come in with karmic patterns of indiscretions but chose to carry imprints, conditioning, and cellular memory to heal familial lineages and to liberate humanity through the healing of myself? Since I was born from a loving Source of perfection, I could only be the perfection of a loving Source. In knowing it is so, I allow frustration, boredom, loneliness, and confusion to be embraced as signs of how rapidly I am expanding, instead of as enemies to oppose, judge, or deny.

While patterns of experiences may repeat, I accept that they only occur for my evolutionary benefit, allowing me to see the same things from higher perspectives of consciousness each and every time. This helps me transform my view of life from spiritual punishment to evolutionary process, where everything is here to help me reach my absolute potential.

And so I am free. And so I am embraced. And so I am redeemed. And so I am fulfilled. And so I am. And so it is.

Throughout this book, we have respected, acknowledged, and welcomed our way into the attributes of the soul's highest qualities. We have begun the process of balancing our inner masculine and feminine energies and embracing the four pillars of self-love to allow our deepest heartfelt surrender to unfold with peace, compassion, and ease. We have come to see the difference between allies and enemies as being a matter of perspective, as we embrace the true meaning of forgiveness by remembering the light of Source energy within and throughout all things.

By honoring the evolutionary benefits encoded in each encounter, our shift from ego to soul continues to evolve in the most heart-centered way. No longer victims of circumstance, we acknowledge the depths of our evolutionary process, as angels in physical form who incarnated to uplift the consciousness of an entire planet.

With each of us making our personal contribution toward the shifting of the collective, we have come to see it's not necessarily a matter of what happens but how we respond that determines our course of mastery.

As these words prepare us to take this wisdom out into the world as faithful companions for our journey ahead, we are to be congratulated on how far we've come and encouraged to continue our expansion as we step across the threshold into the excitement of a brand-new reality.

Welcome home, dear radiant angels. Welcome home.

CHAPTER 13

DAILY
PRACTICES

A SPIRITUAL JOURNEY can be explored on many levels, whether we are a weekend yogi, a casual inquirer, or even a die-hard voyager of our inner reality. Whether we are observing from afar or ready to roll up our sleeves and plunge into the depths of our deepest revelation, it is a journey that requires true commitment in order for the most invaluable insights and experiences to dawn.

Commitment is not to be confused with effort. Oftentimes, effort is determined by how harshly we push, whereas commitment is simply a matter of how consistently we show up. While a willingness to put forth effort is required in many aspects of life, it is important to remember that pushing harder doesn't determine the outcomes we seek, which are often accessed by the earnestness of greater spiritual commitment. Such a commitment isn't a matter of necessarily being good at a particular practice but of perfecting the art of consistent implementation. This means that mastery isn't a goal-oriented achievement of any kind. Without any goals to check off our "spiritual to-do list," mastery becomes a step-by-step celebration of daily attendance.

The value of commitment allows a daily spiritual practice to answer the following questions: How attentive have we learned to become in facing the difficulties in our lives? How often do we attend to our own inner needs, instead of waiting for others to fill the void—or even lashing out when life doesn't go as planned? Have we discovered the true gifts of a spiritual practice as a gift of attendance, where it doesn't matter how talented we are at the practice but how often we show up to meet ourselves at a more intimate and authentic level?

When rooted in true heartfelt commitment, a spiritual practice can offer many benefits to accelerate the evolution of our journey. It can quicken healing time, expand the parameters of limiting perspectives, and even offer greater explanations to the unfolding mysteries within us.

Anytime we have decided to engage in a practice containing positive physical, emotional, or energetic benefit, it is our ability to make time each day for our own self-care and personal growth that allows the value of our highest ethics to expand. If a practice has not been established as a necessary part of our day, we are more likely to be shaken by the uncertain ground of inevitable change.

The more a spiritual practice becomes an established part of our daily routine, the greater harmoniousness we tend to feel, no matter how surprising life becomes. A spiritual practice is not a matter of being good at something. It is simply an exploration into the effort of attendance.

While ego may attempt to perfect each practice or only embrace the processes it believes it can do well, the soul sees a spiritual practice as an opportunity to strengthen the skill set of consistency. The more consistent we are in engaging a practice, the more fulfilling relationships can be created— within and throughout. This is because a spiritual practice is the activity of commitment cultivated through the implementation of consistency. The more consistent we are in our practices, the more we are able to commit ourselves to the giving and receiving of love.

Spiritual practice also helps in healing wounds of abandonment. If we're scarred by memories of rejection, we can help our innocence find emotional resolve through our willingness to commit to a practice and no longer abandon ourselves the way characters from our past have abandoned us. As we dare to commit to our own inner well-being, perhaps with more authenticity and dedication than anyone has ever provided, we strengthen the fiber of our character as an evolving angel in physical form.

It is important to explore a variety of spiritual practices in order to know which one may serve our specific needs. There are times when certain practices resonate, and other times when a practice has run its course. No matter which one is embraced or let go, the purpose is to make time each day for a practice, whether it is the same one for many years or a variety of different ones over a lifetime.

Since the benefits of a spiritual practice often help strengthen one or even all four pillars of self-love, it is common for the ego to feel overwhelmed, stifled, or imprisoned by a process that results in its unraveling. No matter the practice implemented, the ability to become more heart-centered, well-rested, rooted in spaciousness, and at peace with time often occurs as the ego unravels. While the ego attempts to stay intact, hoping to master the very practice that is geared to help it integrate, it is important for us to embrace our spiritual practice with loving-kindness, so the ego can let go with peace and ease.

Spiritual practice is never intended to be used as a weapon against the ego but as an opportunity to make our own evolution and self-care a vital part of our daily experience. Whether we have a good day of practice or feel as if we are fighting every step of the way, it is always a useful means to support greater emotional and energetic harmony as we face the boredom, loneliness, frustration, and confusion that signify the signposts of our deepest inner transformation.

Although the majority of offerings from this book can be utilized as a daily spiritual practice, I wrote this chapter to help synthesize all the teachings into practical application. As always, feel free to embrace the practices that resonate, knowing it's not a matter of trying to do it all but of using this chapter as an extension of your own inner guidance to help find the daily practice that serves your life's highest evolutionary benefit.

Sometimes we may resonate with specific daily practices over a period of time. In other instances, we may be drawn to choosing a different practice each day, week, or month.

Whether you are applying these practices as a personal 90-day challenge or referring to this chapter in search of the perfect remedy for current life circumstances, know that each one has been channeled from the Universe to support your most miraculous transformation.

CULTIVATING WORTHINESS, GRATITUDE, AND PASSION

- PART ONE

I channeled this daily practice to help cultivate worthiness, gratitude, and passion as essential aspects of the soul's expansion. Whether you write in a journal or on a computer, or you recite aloud while in traffic, simply answer the following three questions:

What are three to five things you are grateful for? If nothing arises, what are three to five things you wish you felt grateful for?

No matter how big or small, what are three to five things you have done right today? If nothing arises, what are three to five things you wish you could acknowledge yourself for doing right?

What are three to five things you would love to manifest into your reality? If nothing arises, what are three to five things you would love to manifest for others or even humanity?

As always, feel free to do as little or as much of this practice, however it resonates with you.

CULTIVATING WORTHINESS, GRATITUDE, AND PASSION

– PART TWO

A daily practice of cultivating worthiness, gratitude, and passion can also be applied as a meditation. Whether during walks in nature, when stuck in traffic, or while sitting quietly, fill in the blank in each statement below, then offer a slow mindful inhale and exhale before advancing to the next one. Once you've completed all three statements, repeat the process for 5–15 minutes:

I am grateful for _____.
(Take one slow inhale and exhale.)

I am proud of myself today because I _____.
(Take one slow inhale and exhale.)

I am so excited to manifest _____.
(Take one slow inhale and exhale.)

Even if you're feeling stuck or not genuinely able to complete the following statements, this meditative practice can be adjusted to serve the authenticity of your personal needs:

I wish I were grateful for _____.
(Take one slow inhale and exhale.)

I want to be proud of myself for _____.
(Take one slow inhale and exhale.)

I wish to manifest the worthiness to _____.
(Take one slow inhale and exhale.)

The third option for this meditative practice can be applied whether you're absolutely content in your personal life or so shut down that praying for the well-being of others assists you in finding the proper amount of space to relax and open back up:

May all hearts be grateful for _____.
(Take one slow inhale and exhale.)

May all beings be proud of themselves for _____.
(Take one slow inhale and exhale.)

May the world manifest _____ for the well-being of all.
(Take one slow inhale and exhale.)

Just as in Part One of cultivating worthiness, gratitude, and passion, please allow whichever meditation that best supports your daily experience to be embraced with openness, sincerity, and ease.

THE SWEETNESS GAME

Since the focus of this book is cultivating the RAW qualities of your soul's highest attributes, one of the most effective, nourishing, and transformative ways to be more aligned with Source is to embrace the innate sweetness within yourself and others. This daily practice can be applied as a way of deepening the sweetness of your innocent nature or as an emotional form of resolution in response to personal conflict. Even when the characters in your life don't seem to be operating from the purity of their innocence, you can always use this daily practice as your opportunity to allow any perceivable enemy to become an ally supporting your highest evolution.

To play the Sweetness Game, simply consider each of the following questions and allow whatever answer arises to pop into your mind or bubble up in your heart:

What is the sweetest reason why I am the way I am?

What is the sweetest reason I keep doing what I yearn to change in myself?

What is the sweetest reason why people treat me the way they do?

What is the sweetest reason I am in this current situation?

What is the sweetest reason why the world is the way it is?

What is the sweetest reason why I am here?

If softening your edges to notice the inherent sweetness in all feels too far out of reach, you can simply adjust this daily practice by considering the following questions. Whether answers arise or not, you are always cultivating higher frequencies of light simply by aligning your focus with a more positive and empowered perspective.

What is the most beneficial reason why I am the way I am?

What is the most beneficial reason I keep doing what I yearn to change in myself?

What is the most beneficial reason why people treat me the way they do?

What is the most beneficial reason I am in this current situation?

What is the most beneficial reason why the world is the way it is?

What is the most beneficial reason why I am here?

It is important to remember that a daily practice is *never* intended to justify cruelty. While each practice allows you to see how everything is here to help you, please refrain from using it to perpetuate or maintain victimhood by staying entangled in toxic relationships.

If you happen to find yourself in an environment of abuse, please answer your soul's deepest calling to find a safer environment, while applying each practice as a way of helping yourself heal.

HAND ON YOUR HEART MEDITATION

One of the most effective ways to assist your heart in opening is to spend time with your hand resting on your heart. Because your hands and heart both conduct electrical currents of energy, just by placing your hand on your heart you are sending the electrical charge emanating from your heart back to your heart through the energy flowing through the palm of your hand.

When sitting with your hand on your heart, it doesn't matter how noisy or quiet your mind tends to be, or how good you feel in your body. It is simply a matter of finding pockets of time throughout the day, where you are able to reconnect with yourself, allowing you to be the one who equally receives all the energy you radiate outward for the well-being of all.

This process is beneficial during moments of stress. It is also ideal whenever confronted by the frustration, boredom, loneliness, and confusion of the ego's unraveling. Whether used in response to life's most daunting circumstances or as a way of expanding well-being on an energetic level, your heart tends to feel safe enough to open the more often it feels the power of your loving embrace.

THE POLARITY BLESSING

In order to activate the power of the Polarity Blessing, it is important to remember the potency of our words. Each word is an expression of energy propelled into motion through the power of our consciousness. Throughout each breath, these words can be offered as powerful rays of healing light, just as they can be used as weapons against ourselves and others.

If we dare to put aside any point we attempt to prove, we may ask ourselves, "When not identified with the righteousness of a viewpoint, am I using words as gifts or weapons? How does it feel in my body when I share my words? If it doesn't feel good in my body when conveying my ideas, how do I expect to empower others? For just one moment, can I surrender my need to be right by taking a look at the quality of my words?"

The best way to transform our reality and be a positive source of inspiration for others is to use our words as expressions of freedom and joy. When we are joyful about the words we choose, others around us are likely to get more interested, which gives us the ability to inform and uplift in a conscious, heart-centered way. When joy is forsaken for the ruthlessness and aggression of a personal standpoint, words are used as bully tactics to back others into corners where they are condemned and judged for being different.

All too often, the difference between assembling a social lynch mob and inspiring the hearts of many is the way in which words are used.

As an ongoing daily practice, let each day be an opportunity to compliment and honor the divinity in others, knowing the better others feel about themselves, the more consciousness blossoms throughout the lives of all. If we are unable to use our words as gifts instead of as weapons, we unknowingly exist on the same level of unconsciousness as the things we yearn to change.

If inspired to take even greater conscious action, it is always essential to take action based on what we support, instead of the things we oppose. If this seems less important than the choice to assault through verbal tirades, no amount of words we speak will ever do enough to support the grace of our most important contributions. If we wish to recruit the highest consciousness of all to side with our standpoint, then we dare to conduct ourselves in an honorable, conscious manner.

From this space of heart-centered alignment, consciousness is not determined by the righteousness of our view but by how lovingly we are attempting to share our ideas with others.

As a way of allowing words to be among our most important daily practices, I channeled this blessing from the Universe as a direct way of energetically responding to negative emotions and unfavorable situations. May it offer you more options than you may imagine having during the most insurmountable of circumstances.

The Polarity Blessing was created to help you see the evolutionary benefits in each situation by inviting you to bless yourself and others with the opposite vibration of your most limiting experiences.

This means someone's mistreatment of you can become an opportunity to compliment yourself more often or bless the world with greater self-worth.

Even when criticized by others, you can take a moment to reverse the energy of criticism into a compliment and receive gifts from their souls instead of enduring assaults from their ego.

To assist you in becoming more familiar with the power of the Polarity Blessing, please consider the wisdom of the following questions:

When others are angry or have angered you, what if you blessed yourself and the world with greater happiness?

When others are sad or have saddened you, what if you blessed yourself and the world with greater joy?

When others are shut down or have shut you down, what if you blessed yourself and the world with greater openness?

When others are cruel or have inspired cruelty in you, what if you blessed yourself and the world with greater sweetness?

When others are deceptive or have ignited deception in you, what if you blessed yourself and the world with greater courage to be honest?

When others are disrespectful or have triggered disrespect in you, what if you blessed yourself and the world with greater respect?

When others are in conflict or have engaged in conflict in you, what if you blessed yourself and the world with greater peace?

When others are in pain or have hurt you, what if you blessed yourself and the world with greater healing?

When others feel rejected or have rejected you, what if you blessed yourself and the world with greater acceptance?

When others are in fear or have made you afraid, what if you blessed yourself and the world with greater love?

When others are in judgment or have triggered judgments in you, what if you blessed yourself and the world with greater forgiveness?

THE PRAYER OF RADICAL FORGIVENESS

This teaching and prayer were channeled from the Universe to create a practical tool in response to personal crisis or global turmoil. May it become your first line of response to worldly affairs, as you step forward in service to humanity as an angel on Earth.

The difference between a lightworker and a victim has nothing to do with the situations they face, but with how they *respond* to those situations. A lightworker is an angel in physical form. He or she uses their world of experiences to become the change they wish to see. A victim is hurt by the actions of the world, merely waiting for the change they have yet to become.

On a spiritual level, a victim is a lightworker in training. Throughout each chapter of life, the inevitability of loss and the suchness of change are survived to bring forth a new consciousness for the benefit of all. This means victimhood is not a pitfall to escape but ongoing stages of spiritual growth and energetic expansion to cultivate the lightworker in you.

Whether contracted in fear from the hostility between countries, heartbroken by the actions of terrorist attacks, at war with yourself in your own mind, disappointed by the behavior of a loved one, or overwhelmed by the heaviness of the collective unconscious, each moment of victimhood acts as an invitation to step across the threshold of despair to become the lightworker you are destined to be.

No matter how promising or uncertain your world seems to be, I offer you the prayer of radical forgiveness as a way of assisting our awakening humanity on an energetic level.

It is important to always remember, whether viewing circumstances on a personal or global level, that even if you cannot change the situations you see, you can always change how you respond from the inside out.

As an awakening lightworker on the front lines of ushering humanity into a new paradigm of consciousness, please read the following prayer however many times a day you are either inspired to support in Earth's evolution or find yourself entrenched in the pain of human suffering. In the blank space provided, you can include the name of an enemy, an adversary from the past, a family member connected to a wound you have yet to heal, a loved one struggling through their own healing journey, your full name, the name of a country at war, or even humanity at large.

I allow _____ to be pardoned and set free as I AM now.

Please do not judge yourself for the number of times per day you find yourself needing to repeat this prayer. Instead, see yourself through the eyes of the Universe and rejoice in how often you are acting in accordance with your soul's highest wisdom to transform reality for the liberation of all.

Through the prayer of radical forgiveness, may you step forward in faith and bring to life a unique frequency of light that you came here to ignite in every heart.

May your destiny be viewed not as a horizon of preferred circumstances but as an opportunity to act upon life's most inspired choices that transform your physical body into a living expression of divinity in action.

HEALING WITH GRATITUDE

This teaching and practice was channeled from the Universe as a helpful tool when our healing journeys seem overwhelming or last longer than we desire. May it release you from any sense of self-judgment, so you may further embrace the nature of healing as an evolutionary process.

True healing is not simply a matter of becoming symptom free by any means necessary. That would support beliefs in superstition by suggesting there is no higher purpose for the conditions we are facing. When caught in a healing crisis, our bodies are put into a cocoonlike state, where rest, nourishment, and often the assistance of supplements or even medicine allow the body, mind, heart, and soul to align, get on the same page, and inspire the integration of our highest vibration into physical form.

Most symptoms, whether requiring naturopathic, energetic, or medical attention, symbolize the dying off of the old paradigm as the new self emerges. All too often, before we can sense the fresh horizons of a new reality, we are given the opportunity to thank the old self for taking us as far as it was meant to go, and to send it home to Source.

This can be confusing because so many beings are currently at the precipice of a new reality, yearning to release the old, but it is being done from a space of rejection, where the focus is eliminating the inconveniences that inspire our most profound awakening. When we are able to recognize true healing as nobody's fault, but merely as everyone's *opportunity* to offer gratitude for all the past experiences that have prepared us for greater adventures ahead, we are able to accelerate our healing journey without rejecting any part of ourselves along the way.

Healing is not a race against time to re-create an ego structure under more desirable circumstances; it is an opportunity to embrace self-love, compassion for others, and greater respect for our evolutionary process. Healing is not a matter of trying to figure out what we did wrong in order to manifest such a predicament. It is a time-honored celebration of how quickly we are evolving, where the need for our body, mind, heart, and soul to align causes a variety of symptoms to emerge.

Spiritual healing is not necessarily resolved by modalities nor is any form of medicine less than the path of our highest potential. Whatever your body, mind, heart, and soul require in order to align and integrate is precisely what we should offer ourselves. As always, please trust in the immaculate grace of Divine guidance to know what is best for you. When in doubt, please find more time and space to be still, silent, and open to the guidance that life intends to offer.

May the one who wishes to speed up the process or is only interested in evolution under preferable circumstances be respected, acknowledged, and welcomed as never before. May each stage of healing be savored no matter how exhausting or excruciating it feels as the old paradigm dissolves. As always, our greatest healing remains our deepest surrender. It's not a matter of how long it seems to last but of how willing we are to embrace the vibration of gratitude, whether or not it seems to make an immediate difference.

Once the grace of gratitude helps you acknowledge every moment as a gift of continuous spiritual growth, the pain, losses, uncertainties, betrayals, and heartbreak will still be felt, but it cannot trigger a response of suffering unless gratitude is withheld. In awakened consciousness, pleasure is still pleasurable and pain remains painful. And yet, whether pleasure becomes pain, or pain seems to last longer than we had hoped for, it doesn't diminish our understanding of how invaluable each moment can be to ensure the arrival of our most miraculous expansion.

Best of all, we don't even have to know how something is helping us evolve or envision how much better we'll be as a result of our current climate of conditions. Instead, we can simply receive each moment as an invaluable gift, even if the gift is helping us be totally honest about how much we dislike the way things are.

We don't have to like it. And yet life knows exactly how to mold us into the perfection that we came to live out.

To activate the healing power of gratitude, please consider the wisdom of the following insights, either silently or aloud:

Thank you for this pain.
Thank you for this betrayal.
Thank you for this heartbreak.
Thank you for this inconvenience.

Thank you for this disappointment.
Thank you for this loneliness.

Thank you for this frustration.
Thank you for this agony.
Thank you for this confusion.

Thank you for this disease, illness, or condition.
Thank you for this hopelessness.
Thank you for this anger.
Thank you for this despair.
Thank you for this relentless cruelty.

Thank you for this depression.
Thank you for this humility.
Thank you for this silence.
Thank you for this liberation.
Thank you for this peace.

Thank you for this joy.
Thank you for this light.
Thank you for this life.
Thank you for this love.
Thank you. Thank you. Thank you.

As a daily practice, feel free to read this as often as you wish or in direct response to emotional triggers. You may even wish to read each line to discover which one contains the most emotional discord.

Whichever one creates the most inner tension can become a mantra that you repeat throughout the day to transform any potential enemy of ego into an ally for your soul's evolution.

CONCLUSION

WE'VE COME TO THE END of our journey together—but this is only the beginning of *your journey* forward. You've begun to explore a deeper reality, daring to view your life through the eyes of our all-loving Source, and you have successfully opened yourself up to a wellspring of miracles that serve the unfolding and completion of this lifetime's mission with the utmost peace, harmony, and ease.

While it may not always seem peaceful, harmonious, or easy, the power now rests in *your hands* to determine how many allies or enemies you perceive. From now on, each moment exists as a precious opportunity to be the love you have always desired, and to demonstrate the generosity, consciousness, nobility, and compassion that may seem missing from the world in view. In stepping forward as an active and engaging announcer of well-being, you remind the world of a deeper reality within our human play, simply by the choices you make and the ways you choose to respond. All of which can be uplifting, inspiring, and invigorating, instead of exhausting—if we remember the eternal truth of the new spiritual paradigm. Such a truth dances throughout the ups and downs of everyday life, reminding you that no matter how anything seems or appears—everything is here to help you become the one you were born to be.

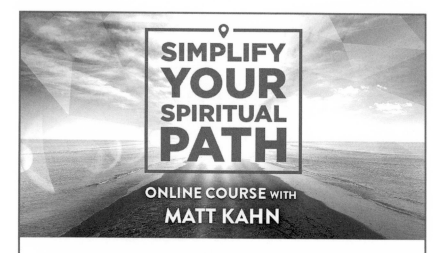

ABOUT THE AUTHOR

MATT KAHN IS A SPIRITUAL TEACHER and highly attuned empathic healer who has become a YouTube sensation with his healing and often humorous videos. His nine million YouTube channel viewers are finding the support they seek to feel more loved, awakened, and open to the greatest possibilities in life.

Matt's spontaneous awakening arose out of an out-of-body experience at the age of eight and through his direct experiences with Ascended Masters and Archangels throughout his life. Using his intuitive abilities of seeing, hearing, feeling, and direct knowing, Matt feels the emotions of others and is able to pinpoint what blocks any heart from opening. As a result, he brings forth revolutionary teachings through both the written and spoken word that assist energetically sensitive beings in healing the body, awakening the soul, and transforming reality through the power of love.

Many spiritual seekers have experienced amazing unexplainable physical and emotional healings and have awakened to their true nature through Matt's profound, loving, and often funny teachings, and transmission of timeless, sacred heart wisdom.

Website: www.MattKahn.org

HAY HOUSE TITLES OF RELATED INTEREST

YOU CAN HEAL YOUR LIFE, the movie,
starring Louise Hay & Friends (available as a 1-DVD program,
an expanded 2-DVD set, and an online streaming video)
Learn more at www.hayhouse.com/louise-movie

THE SHIFT, the movie,
starring Dr. Wayne W. Dyer (available as a 1-DVD program,
an expanded 2-DVD set, and an online streaming video)
Learn more at www.hayhouse.com/the-shift-movie

***

*Adventures of the Soul: Journeys
Through the Physical and Spiritual Dimensions,*
by James Van Praagh

Angel Prayers: Harnessing the Help of Heaven to Create Miracles,
by Kyle Gray

Uncharted: The Journey through Uncertainty to Infinite Possibility,
by Colette Baron-Reid

The Universe Has Your Back: Transform Fear to Faith,
by Gabrielle Bernstein

You Can Create An Exceptional Life,
by Louise Hay and Cheryl Richardson

All of the above are available at your local bookstore,
or may be ordered by contacting Hay House (see next page).

We hope you enjoyed this Hay House book. If you'd like to receive our online catalog featuring additional information on Hay House books and products, or if you'd like to find out more about the Hay Foundation, please contact:

Hay House, Inc., P.O. Box 5100, Carlsbad, CA 92018-5100
(760) 431-7695 or (800) 654-5126
(760) 431-6948 (fax) or (800) 650-5115 (fax)
www.hayhouse.com® • www.hayfoundation.org

———

Published in Australia by:
Hay House Australia Pty. Ltd., 18/36 Ralph St., Alexandria NSW 2015
Phone: 612-9669-4299 • *Fax:* 612-9669-4144 • www.hayhouse.com.au

Published in the United Kingdom by:
Hay House UK, Ltd., Astley House, 33 Notting Hill Gate, London W11 3JQ
Phone: 44-20-3675-2450 • *Fax:* 44-20-3675-2451 • www.hayhouse.co.uk

Published in India by: Hay House Publishers India,
Muskaan Complex, Plot No. 3, B-2, Vasant Kunj, New Delhi 110 070
Phone: 91-11-4176-1620 • *Fax:* 91-11-4176-1630 • www.hayhouse.co.in

———

Access New Knowledge.
Anytime. Anywhere.

Learn and evolve at your own pace
with the world's leading experts.

www.hayhouseU.com

Free e-newsletters
from Hay House, the Ultimate
Resource for Inspiration

Be the first to know about Hay House's free downloads, special offers, giveaways, contests, and more!

 Get exclusive excerpts from our latest releases and videos from *Hay House Present Moments*.

 Our *Digital Products Newsletter* is the perfect way to stay up-to-date on our latest discounted eBooks, featured mobile apps, and Live Online and On Demand events.

 Learn with real benefits! *HayHouseU.com* is your source for the most innovative online courses from the world's leading personal growth experts. Be the first to know about new online courses and to receive exclusive discounts.

 Enjoy uplifting personal stories, how-to articles, and healing advice, along with videos and empowering quotes, within *Heal Your Life*.

Sign Up Now!

Get inspired, educate yourself, get a complimentary gift, and share the wisdom!

Visit www.hayhouse.com/newsletters to sign up today!